THE EVEREST OF INVESTING

THE EVEREST OF INVESTING

GETTING RICH WITH TERMINAL VALUE INVESTING

WRITTEN BY RATTAN JONEJA

The Everest of Investing
Rattan Joneja

Published By CoValue Technologies Pvt. Ltd,
Mumbai, India

First Edition, 2026

Author: Rattan Joneja
Cover design by Saakshi Shetty, 2026

The contents of this book have been certified and timestamped on the Gnosis blockchain as a permanent proof of existence. Scan the QR code or visit the URL given on the back cover to verify the blockchain certification for this book.

ISBN - 978-81-996467-2-8

Disclaimer (Short Form)

This book is for educational and informational purposes only. It does not constitute financial, investment, tax, legal or professional advice. Many data points and examples are presented solely to illustrate broader concepts rather than to provide exhaustive or definitive factual records. Past performance is not indicative of future results; investing involves risk, including possible loss of principal. Readers should conduct independent research and seek guidance from qualified advisers before making decisions.

For a complete statement of terms and limitations, please refer to the full disclaimer at the end of this book.

To Rakesh Jhunjhunwala –

whose vision, conviction, and unwavering belief in India's potential taught us that patience and courage can turn small seeds into mighty forests.

This book is a humble tribute to the Big Bull, who showed the world that the climb to the summit begins with faith in the journey.

Table of Contents

PART II: ENGINES OF COMPOUNDING

PART III: ENDURANCE - THE INVESTOR'S MINDSET

PART IV: LEGACIES, CASE STUDIES & THE FINAL SUMMIT

Preface

The Everest of Investing: A Climb Few Complete

Every investor dreams of finding the next Microsoft, Titan, or Amazon. But in the real world of investing, as in climbing, the discovery is only the first step. The harder challenge is endurance: holding on through drawdowns, doubt, and noise. That's where the true compounding lies.

This book was born from witnessing a base camp moment

In 2002, at a small dinner gathering, Rakesh Jhunjhunwala leaned across the table and, with his trademark conviction, declared:
"Sell everything and buy Titan. Keep it forever."
Back then, Titan traded at barely ₹2 a share (adjusted for splits and bonuses). Today, it has become an 1,800-bagger, but only for those with the patience to weather storms and stay on the climb.

The Everest of Investing is not about stock tips. It is about philosophy. About cultivating the ability to spot early compounders and, more importantly, the mental fortitude to hold them through the long ascent from obscurity to greatness.

Inside, you'll encounter more than twenty legendary companies, chosen not for fashion or fads, but for the clarity of their compounding journeys:

- **Early-stage icons** like Titan, Infosys, Netflix, and Monster Beverage – what their "base camp" looked like, and how they scaled.

- **TAM-redefiners** like Apple, ASML, AutoZone and Booking Holdings, companies that didn't just grow into markets but reshaped them entirely.
- **Moat masters** like FICO, Amazon and HDFC Bank, who built defences strong enough to outlast decades of disruption.
- **Global champions** like Microsoft, NVIDIA, Walmart, Home Depot, Ansys, Eicher Motors (Royal Enfield), Bajaj Finance, and Kweichow Moutai – firms that turned niche strength into towering dominance.
- **Cautionary tales** like BlackBerry, Kodak, and Jet Airways are reminders that not every summit is sustainable.

But companies alone do not climb mountains; investors do. This book also profiles legendary investors who mastered the art of patience:

Buffett, Charlie Munger, Philip Fisher, Peter Lynch, Thomas Russo, Nick Sleep, Li Lu, Rakesh Jhunjhunwala, and Ron Baron. Their stories of discipline and conviction reveal how the greatest fortunes in markets were built not on timing, but on time.

These case studies span industries, continents and market cycles, but they share one unifying theme: they reveal Terminal Value in action.

The structure of this book mirrors the mountain itself. We begin at *base camp*, where ideas are small and uncertain. We climb through the treacherous middle stages of reinvestment and endurance. We explore summits, plateaus, and the rare descents where discipline matters as much as patience. Along the way, you'll find mental models, psychological insights, red flags, and scorecards – tools to make you not just a sharper stock picker, but a steadier long-term thinker.

Terminal Value Investing is not a theory. It is a temperament. A quiet refusal to turn back when the air thins and others retreat.

If you've ever sold too soon, hesitated at the moment of conviction, or missed a life-changing stock because of short-term fears, this book is your map to climbing differently.

Welcome to The Everest of Investing. May it guide you towards patience, conviction, and the compounding peaks few ever reach.

Climb the only peak that matters: patience, conviction, and the path to 100x returns.

This book is for.....;

This book is for investors, fund managers, equity research analysts, investment bankers, CEOs, CFOs, and entrepreneurs who want to understand how true wealth is built – not through speculation, but through the discipline of identifying and holding extraordinary businesses over time. For investors, it offers a roadmap to spotting the rare companies that can compound for decades and shows how to recognise the summit, when growth has peaked and discipline must guide the next move. For CEOs and entrepreneurs, it reveals what truly drives long-term value creation – market size, moats, reinvestment power, and patience – providing lessons on how to build companies that endure and compound wealth for both shareholders and society.

Objectives of the book

The Everest of Investing gives readers a clear framework to identify and hold the rare businesses that can compound into generational wealth. Built on the Four Pillars – Market Size, Moats, Reinvestment Power, and Patience – it explains how to spot companies at base camp, endure the long climb of compounding, and, most importantly, recognise the summit: the stage when growth has peaked and discipline determines whether to hold, reallocate, or exit. Through case studies and timeless lessons from legendary investors, this book offers a roadmap not for chasing markets, but for reaching and stepping wisely from the summit of true value creation.

Acknowledgements

This book represents a synthesis of ideas I have encountered through extensive reading, research, discussions and professional experiences. It makes no claim to originality; the concepts presented here have largely been drawn from the work and wisdom of others, with only limited insights of my own.

I am particularly indebted to the influence of Rakesh Jhunjhunwala, whose perspective and conviction left a lasting impression on my thinking. Equally, I acknowledge the profound intellectual contributions of investors such as Warren Buffett, Peter Lynch, Nick Sleep and many others whose writings and philosophies have shaped the framework of this book. Their visionary thought has provided the foundation upon which this work rests.

I wish to express my heartfelt gratitude to my colleagues at CoValue Technologies Pvt. Ltd., especially Amol Kulkarni and Amol Katarnavare, for their invaluable support in assembling and analysing the data that underpins much of this book.

I am also deeply appreciative of ChatGPT, whose assistance in research, design, and drafting has meaningfully enhanced the clarity, depth, and coherence of this work.

My sincere thanks to Saakshi Shetty for her creative artistry in designing the book's cover and illustrations, and to Harish Mehta for capturing my author portrait with such warmth and precision.

I would also like to thank White Falcon Publishing for their professionalism and attention to detail in editing, formatting, and bringing this book together.

Finally, my deepest gratitude goes to my wife, Seema Joneja, and my son, Raunak Joneja, for their unwavering patience, love, and encouragement throughout this journey. Their faith in me has been the quiet strength behind every page, this book belongs to them as much as it does to me.

PART I

THE CLIMB BEGINS: FOUNDATIONS OF TERMINAL VALUE INVESTING

CHAPTER 1

My Dinner with Rakesh Jhunjhunwala and the Birth of a Lifelong Idea

Compound interest is the eighth wonder of the world. He who understands it, earns it… he who doesn't, pays it.

—***Albert Einstein***

In early 2002, a friend invited me to a small gathering of investors, an intimate setting over good food and wine. Among the guests was Rakesh Jhunjhunwala, already renowned for his uncanny ability to spot companies with massive long-term potential.

As the evening unfolded, everyone was eager for his latest picks. With unshakeable conviction, he offered a single piece of advice:

"Sell everything you own and buy Titan. Keep it forever. This company will create generational wealth."

At the time, Titan traded at about ₹2 per share, adjusted for splits and bonuses. Today, it hovers near ₹3,600, a nearly 1,800-fold return. I'm still amazed by the clarity and confidence he displayed. This wasn't just another tip; it was a lesson in visionary, long-term thinking. Until his passing in 2022, he held onto Titan, a stake that soared to about $1.5 billion.

Imagine standing at the base of Mount Everest, gazing up at a peak that only a handful of climbers ever conquer. Those who do return with tales of courage, glory and immense reward. Investing follows the same pattern. Many never move beyond the foothills, buying and selling with each market tremor. But a select few reach the Everest of investing. These are the people who see what most overlook: Terminal Value.

In 1997, one forward-thinking individual walked into a small bookshop that had just begun selling books online. He did his homework and invested $10,000 in Amazon. Twenty-seven years later, that stake was worth over $7 million. Back then, this venture was barely profitable, making the investment seem risky. Yet it wasn't just another bookshop — it was quietly building the infrastructure for the future of global commerce, something most failed to see.

This book is about identifying the next Titan or Amazon before the rest of the world catches on. It's about finding the rare companies that don't simply grow; they dominate. These aren't flashes in the pan; they're industry-defining giants capable of delivering 100x or even 1,000x returns over time. But to find them, you have to shift your gaze from quarterly numbers to long-term potential, from price to Terminal Value.

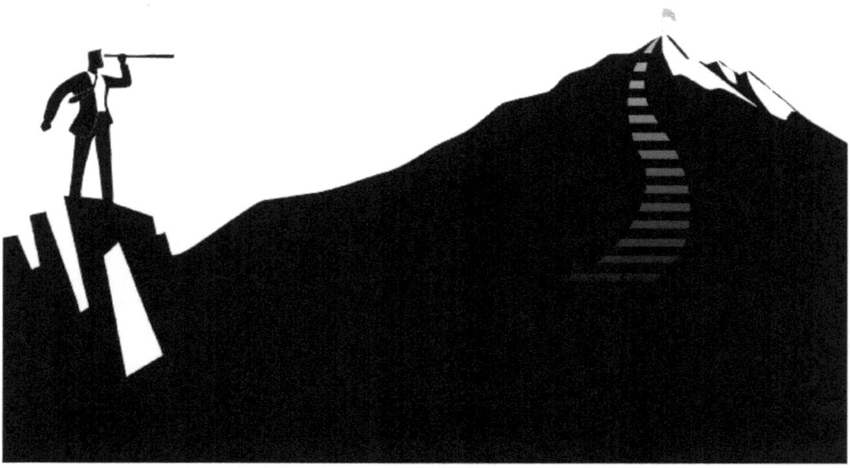

VISION IS THE ART OF SEEING VALUE LONG BEFORE THE MARKET DOES.

What if I told you that finding a 100x stock isn't about perfect timing or insider information, but about understanding one core principle: Terminal Value Investing? Real fortunes come from holding great businesses long enough for compounding to work its magic, not from flipping stocks in search of a quick win.

Welcome to the Everest of Investing. If you're ready to aim higher and leave the small stuff behind, you're in the right place.

What is Terminal Value Investing?

Terminal Value Investing is about investing in companies where the market doesn't discount longevity beyond typical financial forecasts. Instead of just looking at short- to medium-term growth, this approach values a business based on its ability to generate cash flows significantly in the very long term.

Why is Terminal Value Important?

When investors analyse a company, they often forecast its earnings for two, five or ten years. But the cash generation happens in the long term and continues generating cash flows for decades. Terminal value estimates how much the company will be worth after the forecast period.

Why Terminal Value Investing is Like Climbing Everest

Just like climbing Everest, Terminal Value Investing is a long, challenging journey that rewards patience, discipline and resilience. Few reach the summit, just as few investors hold onto 100x stocks long enough to realise their full potential.

- Preparation is Key: Climbers train for years; successful investors study businesses, competitive moats and future cash flows.

- The Climb is Tough: Market downturns and volatility test investors, just as extreme weather and exhaustion test climbers.
- Shortcuts Lead to Failure: Rushing up Everest can be fatal, just like chasing hype stocks without understanding long-term value.
- The Summit is Worth It: Those who endure the journey, holding great companies through decades, reach financial freedom, just as climbers reach the breathtaking Everest summit.

Why Most Investors Fail to Recognise Terminal Value

Most investors fail to grasp Terminal Value because they are trapped in short-term thinking. They focus on quarterly earnings, stock price fluctuations, and short-lived market trends, completely overlooking the long-term compounding power of great businesses.

Here are the key reasons why investors miss out on terminal value:

1. Impatience and Short-Term Bias
   - Investors often expect immediate returns and lack the patience to hold investments for years or decades. This leads to premature selling, cutting off the potential for exponential compounding.
2. Market Noise and Emotional Reactions
   - The financial media constantly bombards investors with news about interest rates, inflation and economic downturns. This distracts them from focusing on a company's long-term fundamentals, causing them to panic sell during volatility.
3. Obsession with Valuation Over Growth
   - Many investors overanalyse short-term valuation metrics (P/E ratios, price-to-book) without understanding the true growth runway of a company. A high-quality business can grow into its valuation over time, delivering massive long-term returns.

4. Failure to Identify Durable Competitive Advantages
    - Terminal value is driven by businesses with strong economic moats, network effects, high switching costs, brand power or technological dominance. Investors often undervalue these moats, focusing instead on short-term profitability.
5. Selling Too Early
    - Even investors who identify great businesses often sell too soon. They take quick profits instead of holding long enough for 100× growth. The biggest gains come from long-term compounding, not short-term flipping.

The Terminal Value Mindset

To truly capitalise on terminal value, investors must shift their mindset:

- Think in decades, not months
- Ignore market noise and short-term volatility
- Identify companies with long-term industry dominance
- Hold through market cycles to allow compounding to work

The investors who understand this principle don't just make money; they build generational wealth.

Investor Takeaways: Climbing the Everest of Terminal Value

1. Great fortunes are built not by buying fast, but by holding long. Rakesh Jhunjhunwala didn't just spot Titan early; he stayed. That decision alone created over $1.5 billion in wealth.
2. The best investments look unimpressive early on.
   Amazon in 1997. Titan in 2002. What made them generational winners wasn't early profitability, but early potential hidden from most, obvious to a few.

3. Terminal Value is where the Everest lies.
   Most of a great company's value lies beyond Year 10. If you sell early, you forfeit the summit for the base camp.
4. Compounding is invisible until it's undeniable.
   A 100x stock doesn't move in a straight line. It tests your patience, convictions and distractions. Those who win are the ones who keep climbing.
5. You must shift from being a stock picker to a business partner.
   Terminal Value Investing means thinking like an owner, studying cash flows, reinvestment, moats and management, not tickers and tips.
6. Everyone gets told about Titan. Few actually buy it. Fewer still hold.
   The Everest is real, but only those with discipline, patience and vision get to plant the flag.

CHAPTER

2

The Four Pillars of Terminal Value Investing

"Time is on your side when you own shares of superior companies."
— ***Peter Lynch***

Great companies and the investments that ride their ascent don't merely spike in value and then fade away. They endure, compounding returns decade after decade on the strength of four timeless principles. In Terminal Value Investing, we distil these principles into four foundational pillars:

- **Market Size**
- **Moats**
- **Reinvestment Power**
- **Patience**

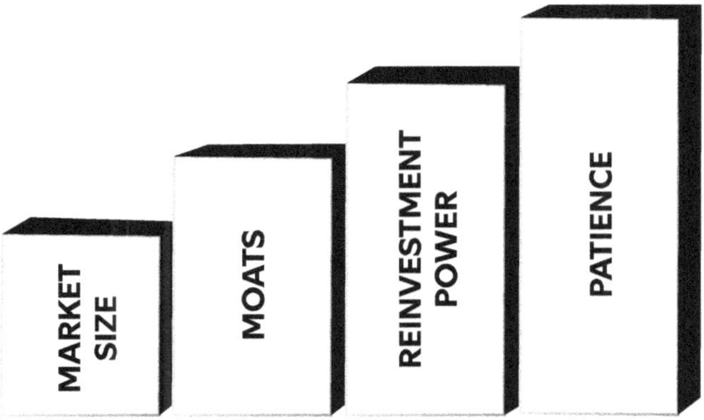

FIND IT. DEFEND IT. REINVEST IT. WAIT.

These aren't abstract theories or tick-the-box metrics; they form the very blueprint behind every 100× success story. Whether it's Amazon expanding from an online bookstore into a global e-commerce, cloud computing and logistics juggernaut, each pillar underpins the journey from base camp to summit.

Why Four Pillars?

Picture attempting to climb Everest with only a single rope, no crampons and no ice axe. Even the strongest climber would stall. Likewise, an investment thesis built on market growth alone and without a durable moat, the ability to reinvest capital or the patience to let compounding run its course will likely falter.

By contrast, truly great businesses combine

1. **Towering Market Size** that unlocks multi-billion-dollar revenue opportunities
2. **Enduring MOATS**, whether distribution networks, brand power, network effects, or economies of scale that ward off competitors
3. **Exceptional reinvestment power** that channels early cash flows into high-return expansion initiatives
4. **Unwavering Patience** in management and shareholders alike, allowing decades-long compounding to work its magic

When these four elements align, they form a virtuous feedback loop: vast markets fuel rapid scale, scale deepens the moat, robust cash flows finance further reinvestment, and time magnifies into outsized returns.

Mapping the Architectural Blueprint

Consider a company entering a $500 billion market with only 1 per cent share – that's already a $5 billion revenue base. But without a moat to defend that share, reinvestment to expand reach, and patience to ride out market cycles, even a large opportunity can slip away. Conversely, businesses that have climbed from humble beginnings to global dominance invariably exhibit all four pillars in concert, creating the rock-solid foundation for compounded growth.

Reflections on the Four Pillars

Terminal Value Investing is not built on prediction. It's built on preparedness. The Four Pillars – Market Size, Moats, Reinvestment, and Patience – offer a timeless lens through which we can evaluate enduring businesses. These pillars don't promise a perfect roadmap, but they provide a compass. They help investors avoid the noise of near-term narratives and anchor themselves to structural truths. And when a company aligns across all four dimensions, the results, while never immediate, can be exponential over time.

To bring these ideas to life, the chapters ahead explore real companies that exemplify one or more of these pillars in action. The businesses selected, from Apple and ASML to Infosys, Moutai, Netflix and Bajaj Finance, are not a definitive list of the world's best investments. Instead, they are illustrative examples chosen for their clarity, diversity and relevance to the framework. The goal is to show how the Four Pillars transcend sectors, borders and business models.

Many other exceptional companies, such as Constellation Software, Mastercard, S&P Global, Divi's Laboratories, Asian Paints, etc., have also demonstrated remarkable long-term performance, including 100× wealth creation. Their exclusion is not a reflection of lesser merit, but a conscious decision to keep the narrative focused. This book does not aim to catalogue every great compounder. It aims to highlight a representative set of them, companies that, in different ways, turned time into their greatest ally.

What Comes Next

With the framework now in place, the rest of this section will unpack each pillar in depth:

- **Chapter 3: Market Size - The Altitude That Defines the Ascent**
  Aiming for markets so vast is the essential first step on the climb.
- **Chapter 4: Moats - Forts Built, Not Found**
  How companies deliberately engineer protective barriers, from distribution networks to network effects, to lock in profits.
- **Chapter 5: Reinvestment Power - Fuelling the Next Wave**
  The art of redeploying early cash flows into high-return projects, R&D and acquisitions to build self-financing growth engines.
- **Chapter 6: Patience - The Hidden Return Multiplier**
  Why true compounding often requires decades and how management culture and investor mindset must align to see strategy through.

Armed with this architectural blueprint, you'll be equipped to identify the enduring compounders – the businesses whose foundations can carry them, and your investment, all the way to the summit. The climb starts now.

In the next chapter, we begin our ascent with the first and perhaps most foundational pillar: Market Size – The Altitude That Defines the Ascent.

CHAPTER 3

Pillar 1 – Market Size: The Altitude That Defines the Ascent

"When a great team meets a lousy market, market wins. When a lousy team meets a great market, market wins. When a great team meets a great market, something special happens."
—***Andy Rachleff, Benchmark Capital (2007)***

Just as Everest climbers study a peak's height and prevailing winds, investors must gauge a company's Total Addressable Market (TAM) to understand its long-term potential. TAM determines whether a business can compound returns for decades or stall at the foothills. Firms with stellar execution but small TAMs may scale quickly yet hit a ceiling. In contrast, companies operating in large, fragmented or expanding markets enjoy both altitude and tailwinds, enabling exponential growth.

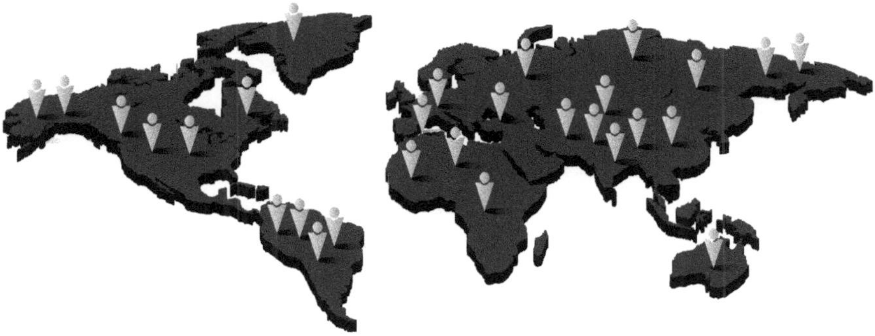

SCALE DEFINES DESTINY.

Moreover, the best companies don't merely grow into markets – they grow with them. They redefine boundaries, unlock adjacent categories, and create platforms that stretch far beyond their starting lines. This chapter is about TAM expansion by design, not accident. Here we spot those climbers who, even after most believe they've summited, keep ascending.

Before we delve into individual case studies, it is important to recognise the three distinct ways companies can expand their total addressable market and hence their long-term runway for growth:

1. Formalizing Fragmented Markets: Bringing structure, branding, and reliability to unorganised sectors (e.g. Titan's Tanishq in India's gold-jewellery market).
2. Adjacent – Category Expansion: Leveraging core capabilities to enter closely related markets (e.g. Amazon's move from books into e-commerce and cloud services).
3. Market Redefinition: Creating entirely new sectors or reshaping the boundaries of existing ones (e.g. Apple's evolution of personal computing into a digital-lifestyle ecosystem).

Each of the companies profiled below has applied one or more of these strategies, finding the altitude and harnessing the wind to power decades of compounding. Now, let's examine how their TAMs grew from **"Base Camp"** to the summit.

Microsoft: From Desktop Software to Cloud Sovereignty

At the time of its 1986 IPO, Microsoft operated in a nascent packaged software market, primarily operating systems and basic productivity tools, estimated at just US $3 billion. That year, it posted revenues of $197 million. By the early 1990s, as personal computing accelerated, the PC software market expanded to ~$10 billion, propelled by

MS-DOS, Windows, and the rollout of Microsoft Office, which itself added another $5–7 billion as businesses digitised core workflows.

Over the next three decades, Microsoft scaled successive peaks of addressable market expansion:

- Productivity & Business Processes: Evolved into an $85+ billion segment powered by Office 365, Teams, and Dynamics.
- Intelligent Cloud: Anchored by Azure, now competes in a $750 billion global cloud market expected to surpass $2.4 trillion by 2030, driven by AI, machine learning, and data infrastructure.
- Strategic Acquisitions: LinkedIn, GitHub, Nuance, and Activision Blizzard extended Microsoft's reach into enterprise networking, developer ecosystems, healthcare AI, and gaming, each unlocking new TAM frontiers.

Today, Microsoft's total addressable market comfortably exceeds $1.5 trillion, with cloud, AI and enterprise SaaS platforms driving the next phase of growth.

In FY2025, Microsoft reported revenues of $281 billion, marking a 20% CAGR since 1986. Its TAM has expanded at a similar trajectory (~18% CAGR), illustrating how a desktop software pioneer has continually reinvented itself atop the world's evolving digital infrastructure.

Titan: Formalising India's Gold Jewellery Frontier

In 2001, India's gold jewellery market was worth around US $7.5 billion and over 96% unorganised. Titan had entered this market with a clear thesis: trust would be the decisive growth driver. Through its Tanishq brand, Titan brought showroom standardisation, transparent karat-based pricing, and rigorous purity checks to a sector still dominated by informal goldsmiths. This professionalised the buying experience and catalysed the shift to branded retail.

Over the next two decades, India's organised jewellery segment grew nearly twelvefold to an estimated US$90 billion by 2025, a TAM CAGR of ~11%. Titan's revenues expanded in step, from ₹639 crore in FY2001 to ₹60,456 crore in FY2025 (~21% CAGR over 24 years). Even today, 60–65% of the market remains unorganised, giving Titan significant headroom to keep scaling in a growing, formalising industry.

Amazon: A $12.4 Billion Niche to a $6 Trillion+ Opportunity

In 1997, Amazon began as a focused online bookstore targeting a US $12.4 billion U.S. market. But Jeff Bezos envisioned a platform that could capture multiple massive addressable markets. By relentlessly reinvesting into fulfilment centres, AWS infrastructure, Prime membership, and digital advertising, Amazon expanded its reach from books to global e-commerce, cloud computing, subscription media, and online advertising. The TAM now exceeds US $6 trillion in combined potential.

From just US $147 million in revenue in 1997, Amazon grew to US $637 billion in 2024, compounding at ~36% annually. Its TAM expanded almost as fast—~ 25% annually, driven by underpenetrated sectors that Amazon actively helped formalise and scale. This is market size expansion in its purest form: growing the mountain while climbing it.

HDFC Bank: Formalising India's Retail Banking

When HDFC Bank launched in the late 1990s, India's formal credit market was just ₹3.5 lakh crore in 1998, reaching fewer than 10% of households. Financial access was largely dominated by public sector banks with limited customer-centric innovation. By pioneering digital account opening, efficient retail lending, and disciplined NPA management, HDFC Bank helped expand financial inclusion and accelerate the adoption of electronic payments.

These forces widened India's total addressable banking market to an estimated ₹27 lakh crore by 2024, compounding at ~8% annually. Over the same period, HDFC Bank's income grew from ₹302 crore in 1998 to ₹4,70,915 crore in 2025, a ~31% CAGR. Much of this growth came from steadily capturing share from public sector banks, whose dominance fell from 81% in 1998 to 59% in 2024. The market itself was expanding, but HDFC Bank ensured it captured more than its fair share of the ascent.

Apple's Expanding TAM

In the early 2000s, Apple was a niche player in a ~$180 billion global PC market. The iPod's 2001 launch marked a turning point, propelling Apple beyond computing into consumer-centric innovation. With iTunes (2003), Apple created a digital marketplace that expanded its role from hardware into media distribution. The inflection came in 2007 with the iPhone, which disrupted the $180 billion smartphone industry and redefined how users interact with technology.

Apple didn't stop there. The App Store (2008), Apple Watch, AirPods, iCloud, Apple Music, and Apple Pay expanded its TAM across wearables, payments, content, and health. By 2024, Apple's addressable markets exceeded $1.5 trillion, whilst revenues compounded at ~17% annually from $5.3 billion (2001) to $391 billion (2024). Apple didn't just ride market growth; it created it, turning functional markets into cultural movements and redefining TAM as a dynamic, expanding frontier.

That transformation from device-maker to ecosystem giant perfectly illustrates the power of TAM reinvention and Terminal Value Investing in action.

Kweichow Moutai: From an $18 Billion Spirits Niche to a $155 Billion+ Baijiu Empire

In 2001, China's premium spirits market was a relatively niche $18 billion category, dominated by state-owned producers and opaque distribution. Kweichow Moutai stood apart as the national liquor, steeped in heritage, cultural prestige, and political symbolism. Its unique positioning meant it wasn't simply alcohol, but a marker of status, corporate gifting, and diplomatic currency.

As China's middle class expanded and national pride surged, demand for premium baijiu multiplied. By 2023, Moutai's TAM had surpassed $155 billion, compounding at nearly 10% annually. Revenue scaled from $220 million in 2002 to $24.8 billion in 2024 (≈24% CAGR), with industry-leading margins. What began as a niche domestic market transformed into one of the world's largest luxury consumption categories, redefined by Moutai's cultural capital and brand power.

Infosys Market Size: From Outsourcing Niche to a $600B+ Opportunity

In 1993, Infosys's breakthrough came with a landmark dedicated outsourcing centre contract from GE, its entry into what was then a ~$76 billion global IT services market. This was the beginning of India's offshoring revolution, where cost efficiency, talent scale, and quality certification allowed companies like Infosys to capture global demand.

Over time, Infosys expanded well beyond cost arbitrage. It invested early in digital transformation, cloud, cybersecurity, and AI-powered platforms — aligning itself with evolving enterprise priorities. By 2025, Infosys was competing in a \$600+ billion Global IT Outsourcing market. Revenues scaled from ₹257 crore in FY1998 to ₹162,990 crore in FY2025, a ~27% CAGR over 27 years. What began as a niche outsourcing partner became a trusted transformation engine for the world's largest corporations.

ASML: From a \$4 Billion Niche to a \$42.8 Billion Semiconductor Backbone

In 1995, ASML was a niche player in the \$4 billion lithography tools market, an essential but relatively obscure corner of the semiconductor value chain. As transistor scaling continued and Moore's Law approached physical limits, demand for precision lithography grew exponentially.

By betting on Extreme Ultraviolet (EUV) lithography, ASML positioned itself at the centre of an industry that ballooned to \$42.8 billion+ by 2024 (≈8.5% CAGR). Over the same period, ASML's revenue grew from \$572 million in 1995 to \$28 billion in 2024, compounding at ~14% annually. What began as a niche photolithography vendor became the linchpin of a multi-trillion-dollar semiconductor economy, enabling smartphones, AI and high-performance computing to flourish.

NVIDIA: From a \$100B GPU Market to a \$1T+ AI Ecosystem

In 2012, the computer graphics hardware market was worth ~\$100 billion, establishing Nvidia in gaming and visualisation. Over the next decade, Nvidia expanded well beyond GPUs for gamers, reinvesting in AI, deep learning and data centre solutions.

By 2022, the company projected its total addressable market at over \$1 trillion, spanning accelerated computing, hyperscale data centres, autonomous vehicles, robotics, and edge computing, growing at ~26% annually. Financially, Nvidia's revenue soared from $5 billion in FY2016 to $130 billion in FY2025, a ~43% CAGR. What began as a gaming chip vendor became the backbone of AI infrastructure, powering the most transformative technology trends of the century.

AutoZone: From a $24 Billion DIY Niche to a $468 Billion Aftermarket Powerhouse

In the mid-1990s, AutoZone operated in the $24 billion U.S. "Do-It-Yourself" (DIY) auto parts segment, serving individual car owners seeking affordable maintenance. This niche sat within a much larger $188 billion U.S. aftermarket. AutoZone's genius lay in identifying growth beyond DIY, expanding into the "Do-It-For-Me" (DIFM) segment, which served garages, repair shops and fleets.

By combining its retail scale with commercial programmes, digital supply chains, and proprietary products like Duralast, AutoZone grew into a critical infrastructure player for the full spectrum of vehicle servicing. Today, the company participates in a $468 billion+ global aftermarket, nearly 20× larger than its original niche. Revenues mirrored this growth, compounding from $1.8 billion in 1995 to $18 billion in 2025 (~8% CAGR over three decades).

Netflix: From a $2.8 Billion DVD Niche to a $575 Billion Global OTT Market4

In 2002, the U.S. DVD-by-mail and rental market stood at just $2.8 billion, dominated by Blockbuster and other physical-rental giants. Netflix, then a niche disruptor, generated only $150 million, barely 7–8% of the market. But its leadership thought bigger. Betting early on rising internet bandwidth and shifting viewing habits, Netflix pivoted towards streaming, transforming itself from a mail-order service into the company that redefined how the world consumes media.

Global over-the-top (OTT) entertainment surged alongside Netflix's pivot, compounding at nearly 27% annually to exceed $575 billion by 2024. Netflix's own revenues grew in tandem, from $152 million in 2002 to $39 billion in 2024, a 29% CAGR over two decades. This expansion illustrates a core principle of Terminal Value Investing: the greatest compounders are those that not only participate in large addressable markets but actively expand and shape them.

Monster Beverage: From a $2 Billion Energy-Drink Category to an $80 Billion+ Global Beverage Market

In 2002, energy drinks were a $2 billion niche, barely registering against the giants of fizzy drinks and sports beverages. Monster, then a scrappy challenger with just $92 million in revenue, staked its future on rebellious branding and youth culture. By 2015, its strategic partnership with Coca-Cola secured global shelf space and supply-chain muscle, allowing it to tap into international demand. By 2024, the energy drink category had exploded to over $80 billion, compounding at ~18% annually. Monster's revenues mirrored this trajectory, growing to $7 billion — a 22% CAGR over two decades, illustrating how small, overlooked niches can become global markets when paired with the right execution.

Home Depot: From Warehouse Upstart to Industry Shaper

When Home Depot went public in 1985, the US home-improvement market was worth roughly $80.3 billion, a fragmented space dominated by mum-and-pop stores. By introducing the big-box warehouse format, Home Depot expanded the addressable market, transforming a patchwork of small vendors into a scalable, formal retail category. The US home improvement industry grew into a $574 billion category by 2024 (~5% CAGR), with Home Depot at the centre. Its revenues surged from $430 million in 1985 to $157 billion in 2024 (16% CAGR), proving how TAM expansion through format innovation drives long-term compounding.

Walmart: From Small-Town Stores to Global Retail Giant

By the mid-1970s, Walmart was a regional discounter operating in a $156 billion core U.S. merchandise market within a $577 billion retail economy. Its strategy of scale-driven logistics and Supercenters didn't just capture share; it expanded the category itself. By 2024, U.S. retail had grown to $6.5 trillion (8% CAGR), while Walmart's revenues climbed to $680 billion from $230 million in 1975, a 17% CAGR since its IPO in 1975. From rural Arkansas to over 10,500 stores worldwide, Walmart exemplifies how relentless TAM expansion, powered by logistics and format evolution, creates multi-decade compounding machines.

Ansys: From a $1.6 Billion Simulation Niche to a $10 Billion+ Engineering Platform

At the turn of the century, Ansys operated in a niche market of global simulation software which was valued at just US $1.6 billion. But as product complexity accelerated and research and development expenses surged across sectors like aerospace, automotive, and industrial machinery, simulation moved from optional to essential.

Ansys capitalised on this shift. By 2024, its addressable market had grown to over US $16.6 billion, expanding at an annual rate of nearly 10%. Over the same 24 years, Ansys's own revenues rose from US $77 million in 2000 to US $2.5 billion, compounding at ~16% annually. What began as a specialist tool evolved into a mission-critical engineering platform, rooted in accuracy, simulation depth, and long-term reinvestment discipline.

FICO: From $4.6B Credit Scoring to $109B Analytics & Decisioning Platform

In 2002, FICO's core addressable market consisted of roughly US $4.59 billion in credit-scoring services. Over the ensuing two decades, it broadened into fraud detection, advanced analytics, and decision-management solutions for banks, insurers, and merchants, expanding its TAM to approximately US $109 billion today, compounding at 16% CAGR. During that span, FICO's revenue climbed from US $0.298 billion in 2000 to US $1.71 billion in 2024, reflecting an 8% compound annual growth rate.

Eicher Motors: Expanding the Altitude of Aspiration

In 2008, India's two-wheeler market stood at ~$6 billion, but the mid-sized motorcycle segment (250–750cc) remained a niche, dominated by overpriced imports and legacy models. Royal Enfield, under Eicher Motors, disrupted this space with vintage styling, thumping engines, and an identity rooted in Indian culture. The two-wheeler TAM grew at a CAGR of 8% to $22 billion.

Instead of pursuing mass market volume or cutting-edge tech, Royal Enfield built a lifestyle brand, one driven by emotion, community, and aspirational riding. As the mid-sized motorcycle segment scaled up over 17 years, Royal Enfield's revenues rose from ₹255 crore to ₹16,536 crore, compounding at an impressive 28% annually.

Crucially, this wasn't just about capturing demand; it was about creating it. Royal Enfield redefined what premium biking meant in India. It's a textbook example of TAM expansion, where vision, identity, and execution fuse to unlock long-term terminal value.

Booking Holdings: From a $19 Billion Foothill to a $566 Billion Summit

At the dawn of the millennium, only 4% of the world's $476 billion travel spend was online, leaving Priceline with a narrow $19 billion digital niche. Its opaque 'name-your-own-price' flights barely scratched the surface, and the stock collapsed after the dot-com bust, a reminder that great execution means little without a vast market to scale into.

The turning point came in 2005 with the acquisition of Booking.com for $133 million, opening access to Europe's fragmented hotel sector and expanding Priceline's online opportunity to ~$175 billion. Over the next two decades, broadband, smartphones and search advertising pushed more travel activity online. Priceline evolved into Booking Holdings, adding rental cars, Agoda and KAYAK, and perfecting a performance marketing flywheel that recycled every booking into growth.

By 2024, online travel had swelled to $566 billion, over 60% of global travel spend. Booking processed more than 1 billion room nights and generated $23.7 billion in revenue, up from $1.2 billion in 2000 (~13% CAGR). Its stock surged from $17.68 in 2003 to over $5,700, a 323× return. This ascent shows how spotting under-penetrated markets early and scaling as they expand defines terminal value.

Bajaj Finance: Climbing with an Expanding Credit Horizon

In 2010, India's retail credit market was still in its infancy, credit to GDP hovered around 10%, and formal lending was largely confined to salaried urban households. NBFCs faced high funding costs, weak data availability, and poor underwriting standards. Against this backdrop, Bajaj Finance, then a small two-wheeler financier, made a decisive pivot. Instead of competing head-on with banks, it focused on underpenetrated niches, leveraging early investments in data-driven risk pricing, technology, and customer segmentation.

From this low-altitude base, India's NBFC retail credit AUM grew from ₹1.85 lakh crore in 2010 to ₹22 lakh crore in 2025 (~18% CAGR). Bajaj Finance was more than a participant; it became a catalyst. Its income surged from ₹910 crore in 2010 to ₹69,683 crore in 2025 (~33% CAGR). By using EMI cards, credit bureau partnerships, and digital origination, it tapped customer segments banks overlooked and adapted quickly to fintech disruption, demonstrating how spotting a vast but underdeveloped TAM and scaling patiently can yield multi-decade compounding.

Conclusion

The tables below synthesise two critical dimensions of long-term growth:

1. TAM Growth: How each firm's Total Addressable Market expanded from its "Base Camp" year to its current peak. This metric illustrates not just the market opportunity they initially targeted, but how visionary strategies, whether formalising fragmented industries, creating adjacent categories, or redefining entire sectors, multiplied their addressable horizons over time.
2. Sales CAGR: The compound annual growth rate in revenues, reflecting how effectively each company transformed market potential into realised sales. High CAGRs indicate businesses that not only identified large and expanding markets but also executed with operational excellence and relentless reinvestment.

Together, these tables provide a quantitative roadmap of how the world's most enduring compounders climbed from modest footholds to market leadership, charting both the altitude of opportunity and the pace of ascent.

Table 1: From Base Camp to Summit: TAM Growth Stories

Company	Base Year	TAM Then	TAM Now	TAM CAGR
Microsoft	1986	$3 B	$1.5 T	18%
Titan	2001	$7.5 B	$90 B	11%
Amazon	1997	$12.4 B	$6 T+	25%
HDFC Bank	1998	₹3.5L Cr	₹27 L Cr	8%
Apple	2001	$180 B	$1.5 T+	10%
Kweichow Moutai	2003	$18 B	$155 B	10%
Infosys	1998	$76 B	$600 B	8%
ASML	1995	$4 B	$42.8 B+	8.5%
NVIDIA	2012	$100 B	$1 T+	26%
AutoZone	1995	$118 B	$468 B+	5%
Netflix	2002	$2.8 B	$575 B+	27%
Monster	2002	$2 B	$80 B+	18%
Home Depot	1985	$80.3 B	$574 B+	5%
Walmart	1975	$156 B	$6.5 T	8%
Ansys	2000	$1.6 B	$16.6 B	10%
FICO	2002	$4.6 B	$109 B	16%
Eicher Motors	2008	$6 B	$22 B	8%
(2 Wheeler) Booking Holdings	2000	$19 B	$566 B	15%
Bajaj Finance	2010	₹1.85 Cr	₹22LCr	18%

Table 2: Sales CAGR Overview

Company	Currency	Base Year	Base Year Revenue	Current Year	Current Revenue	Sales CAGR
Microsoft	$	Jun-86	0.197 B	Jun-25	281 B	20%
Titan	₹	Mar -01	639 Cr	Mar -25	60456 Cr	20.9%
Amazon	$	Dec -97	0.147 B	Dec -24	637 B	36%
HDFC Bank	₹	Mar-98	302 Cr	Mar-25	470,915 Cr	31%
Apple	$	Sep-01	5.3B	Sep-24	391 B	21%
Kweichow Moutai	$	Dec-02	0.22 B	Dec-24	25.8 B	24%
Infosys	₹	Mar-98	257 Cr	Mar-25	162,990 Cr	27%
ASML	$	Dec-95	0.572 B	Dec-24	28 B	14%
NVIDIA	$	Jan-16	5 B	Jan-25	130 B	43%
AutoZone	$	Aug-95	1.8 B	Aug-24	18 B	8.2%
Netflix	$	Dec-02	0.152 B	Dec-24	39 B	29%
Monster	$	Dec-02	0.092 B	Dec-24	7 B	22%
Home Depot	$	Jan-85	0.43B	Feb-25	157 B	16%
Walmart	$	Jan-75	0.23B	Jan-25	680 B	17%
Ansys	$	Dec-00	0.077 B	Dec-24	2.5 B	16%
FICO	$	Sep-00	0.298 B	Sep-24	1.71 B	8%
Eicher Motors	₹	Mar-08	255 Cr	Mar-25	16536 Cr	28%
(2 Wheeler) Booking Holdings	$	Dec-00	$1.2 B	Dec 24	23.7 B	13%
Bajaj Finance.	₹	Mar-10	910 Cr	Mar-25	69683 Cr	33%

Key Investor Takeaways

Climbing Everest demands not only fortitude but the right route, favourable winds, and accurate altitude gauges. Likewise, identifying 100× compounders requires evaluating whether the market itself has the altitude and tailwinds to sustain decades of compounding:

1. Altitude Matters: Always assess TAM's size and growth potential; small TAMs cap ultimate returns.
2. Wind at Your Back: Seek companies that expand, redefine, or invent markets, not just capture share.
3. Paths to Expansion: Direct category share, adjacent verticals, or radical market redefinition.
4. Enduring Ascent: True compounders build systems, reshape demand, and reinvest relentlessly to keep climbing.

In the Everest of Investing, your first question isn't **"When to buy?" but "Where to climb?"** Choose a peak with both altitude and wind, and you'll be on the path to summit the greatest wealth-creation opportunities.

CHAPTER

4

Pillar 2 - Moats is What Keeps You on the Mountain

"The most important thing in evaluating businesses is figuring out how big the moat is around the business. I want to know how big the capital is on the inside and then I want to know how big the moat is around it. What you love is big capital and a big moat"

— *Warren Buffett*

If Total Addressable Market defines how high a company can climb, moats determine how long it can stay there. A moat is a self-reinforcing competitive advantage that deepens with scale and reinvestment, one that shows up over time in widening margins, unshakeable customer loyalty and pricing power. In Terminal Value Investing, moats aren't cosmetic; they are functional barriers that protect profits and preserve market share for decades.

GOLDEN TOWERS RISE ONLY WHEN MOATS HOLDS STRONG.

Competitive Moats in Action

Microsoft: Ecosystem & Enterprise Lock-In

Microsoft's moat is built on a vast software and cloud ecosystem deeply embedded in global enterprises. From Windows and Office 365 to Azure and GitHub, Microsoft creates high switching costs at every layer of IT infrastructure. Its tools are integrated into workflows, collaboration, security and development pipelines, making migration costly, complex and often unnecessary. The result: a self-reinforcing enterprise franchise.

Titan: Brand & Retail Scale

In a market long plagued by purity scams and opaque pricing, Titan institutionalised trust. Tanishq's consistent showroom experience, transparent carat pricing, and certified quality guarantees reshaped customer expectations. Backed by Tata's reputation, the brand built deep loyalty that competitors struggle to replicate.

Vertical integration, from in-house design to manufacturing to controlled retail, ensures quality, speeds product launches, and protects margins. The nationwide network of prime-location showrooms compounds this moat: each new store reinforces brand visibility, lowers per-unit marketing costs, and enhances customer convenience, further widening the gap from regional jewellers.

Amazon: The Infrastructure Layer of Digital Commerce

Amazon's early bets on fulfilment infrastructure, Prime membership, and AWS forged a self-reinforcing flywheel. Faster delivery increased customer loyalty, which attracted more third-party sellers, improving selection and pricing. More sellers meant more choice, which drew even more customers, locking both sides of the marketplace into Amazon's ecosystem.

AWS added a second moat: global cloud infrastructure with high switching costs and deep integration into customer operations. Together, these moats make Amazon not just a retailer but a platform upon which other businesses depend, hard to replicate and harder to disrupt.

HDFC Bank: Execution Culture as a Moat

HDFC Bank's most enduring advantage has been its culture of disciplined execution. Relentless focus on underwriting quality, technology-driven processes, and conservative risk management produced industry-low NPAs across cycles. This consistency, paired with customer-centric service, created trust barriers that new entrants and even established rivals struggled to breach.

Its ability to scale while preserving asset quality made the bank the benchmark for Indian retail finance. The moat was not a single factor, but an operating culture institutionalised across branches, processes and management layers replicated year after year, ensuring compounding without collapse.

Apple's Ecosystem Lock-In

Apple's moat rests on deep integration across hardware, software and services. Each device, whether iPhone, iPad or Mac, plugs seamlessly into the iCloud-driven ecosystem, reinforced by the App Store, iMessage, FaceTime and Apple Pay. Customers build libraries of apps, media and accessories, raising switching costs with every purchase.

Brand loyalty strengthens this moat further. Apple's design excellence, customer service through Apple Stores, and cultural status as a lifestyle brand create stickiness beyond utility. Beneath the surface, its global supply chain mastery, precision manufacturing, materials sourcing, and just-in-time logistics ensure consistency and quality at scale. Together, these layers form a competitive fortress where integration, habit, and trust converge.

Kweichow Moutai: Cultural Prestige and Scarcity Moat

Moutai's moat is inseparable from Chinese tradition and national pride. It is the official state banquet spirit and has been presented as a diplomatic gift since the Mao era. Unlike competitors who rely on advertising, Moutai derives dominance from cultural embeddedness and scarcity.

The company enforces strict production quotas, creating structural scarcity. Its controlled distribution network, backed by government oversight, enforces pricing discipline, with violators permanently delisted. This scarcity elevates Moutai to a luxury asset: bottles are often gifted, collected, or even traded like fine art. In the premium spirits market, this heritage-driven scarcity moat is nearly impossible to replicate, cementing Moutai's monopoly-like position.

Infosys: Client Stickiness and Delivery Discipline

Infosys's moat is built on execution reliability and embedded client relationships. By pioneering the global delivery model, splitting work between on-site teams abroad and offshore centres in India, it created a cost-effective, scalable template for IT services. This model made Infosys integral to client technology roadmaps.

Switching costs grew as Infosys accumulated long-term relationships, proprietary frameworks, and industry-specific expertise. Certifications like SEI-CMM Level 5 reinforced its reputation as the gold standard for process quality. Over decades, one-off projects evolved into multi-year, multi-billion-dollar engagements, creating durable stickiness and defending margins in a competitive industry.

ASML: The Unbreachable Fortress of EUV

ASML holds one of the strongest moats in modern industry: monopoly control of EUV lithography. Its machines, priced at over $150 million each, are indispensable for producing the world's most advanced chips. No competitor has matched ASML's decades of accumulated know-how, protected by deep intellectual property, intricate engineering and unrivalled supply chain mastery.

For TSMC, Samsung, and Intel, there is no alternative; ASML's tools are mission critical. The company doesn't just sell hardware; it sells access to the future of computing. Its moat is reinforced by lock-in effects, as customers co-develop roadmaps alongside ASML, ensuring long-term reliance on its ecosystem. The result: royalty-like margins and a competitive fortress that is practically unassailable.

NVIDIA: Architectural & Ecosystem Dominance

Nvidia's moat extends beyond fast chips into a self-reinforcing ecosystem. Its proprietary CUDA platform became the default language for parallel computing, embedding Nvidia hardware into AI, HPC, and scientific research workflows. Developers, researchers, and enterprises invested years of work into CUDA libraries and models, raising high switching costs.

Each new GPU generation reinforced Nvidia's performance lead, while its software stack (CUDA, cuDNN, TensorRT) deepened developer lock-in. Partnerships with hyperscalers, AI pioneers, and OEMs expanded its reach into every compute-intensive industry.

This combination of hardware leadership and software stickiness created an unbreachable moat, anchored not just in silicon, but in habits, tools, and codebases that competitors struggle to replicate.

AutoZone: Footprint, Inventory, and DIFM Services

AutoZone's moat rests on its vast physical footprint, dense inventory, and integrated DIFM service model. With thousands of locations across North America, the company ensures rapid parts availability, expert guidance, and reliable service for both DIY and professional customers.

Each store strengthens AutoZone's hub-and-spoke distribution model, enhancing logistical efficiency and scale. Exclusive supplier agreements and proprietary brands like Duralast deepen differentiation, while high-frequency DIFM orders embed AutoZone into the daily operations of repair shops. This combination of physical scale, logistical precision, and customer loyalty forms a durable moat that competitors struggle to match.

Netflix: The Content & Data Flywheel

Netflix's moat rests on a self-reinforcing loop of proprietary content and data. Its recommendation engine, built on granular user viewing behaviour, informs not only what content users see but also what content Netflix produces. This personalisation makes discovery seamless, deepens engagement, and raises switching costs.

As scale grew, the flywheel strengthened: more subscribers generated richer data, which guided more effective content investments, which attracted still more subscribers. Originals like House of Cards, Stranger Things, and The Crown became global cultural touchpoints. For competitors, matching Netflix's blend of personalisation, brand,

and cultural relevance has proven enormously costly, cementing its moat as both technological and emotional.

Monster Beverage: Lifestyle Brand + Coca-Cola Distribution Monster's moat lies in the rare combination of authentic lifestyle branding and mass-market reach. Rooted in extreme sports, gaming and music, Monster cultivated cultural credibility that Red Bull couldn't replicate. The 2015 Coca-Cola partnership gave Monster unmatched distribution scale, putting its cans on shelves from Tokyo to Texas. This blend of underground identity and global reach created a brand-and-distribution moat that competitors find nearly impossible to copy.

Home Depot: Scale, Supply Chain & Professional Services

Home Depot's moat rests on scale-driven convenience and operational precision. Its big-box stores serve as both warehouses and fulfilment hubs, offering everything from lumber to professional installation under one roof. Sophisticated supply chains, centralised distribution, and Pro Services for contractors lock in repeat business. This integration of retail scale, logistics efficiency, and professional loyalty creates a moat that secures Home Depot's dominance in home improvement.

Walmart: The Everyday Low-Price Fortress

Walmart's enduring moat is its structural ability to deliver 'Everyday Low Prices'. Its massive purchasing power, dense store network and advanced logistics system give it a cost base competitors can't match. Rivals must either sacrifice margins or cede market share. Walmart has effectively weaponised efficiency: its moat lies not just in offering lower prices, but in having the structural margin to sustain them indefinitely.

Ansys: Embedded in the DNA of Engineering

Ansys sits at the core of mission-critical design workflows across aerospace, automotive, and industrial sectors. Its simulation engines are not optional tools but essential infrastructure, trusted for accuracy, reliability, and breadth of physics. Once integrated, replacing Ansys is prohibitively costly: teams would need retraining, models would need rewriting, and systems would need revalidation. This creates a moat of extremely high switching costs. For engineers, Ansys isn't just software; it is the invisible backbone of innovation, a position few competitors can challenge.

FICO: The Indispensable Backbone of Credit Analytics

FICO operates less like a software vendor and more like a public utility. Its scoring algorithms are embedded into underwriting workflows, regulatory frameworks, and institutional decision-making worldwide. Replacing it would mean revalidating decades of historical credit data and navigating complex regulatory approval processes, an impractical task for most banks and lenders. Its moat rests on three pillars: proprietary data relationships, regulatory entrenchment, and unmatched historical performance. In credit analytics, FICO is indispensable infrastructure.

Royal Enfield: A Brand Moat Forged in Aspiration

Royal Enfield turned motorcycles into more than machines; it made them symbols of belonging. With retro styling, the signature thump of its engines, and a lifestyle ecosystem built around riding clubs, flagship stores and community events, it created emotional equity few rivals could replicate.

This wasn't simply a response to demand but the creation of it. Riders didn't buy Royal Enfields for utility; they bought into an identity. That brand-led loyalty translated into pricing power, repeat customers, and a moat rooted not in engineering alone, but in culture. In India's mid-sized motorcycle market, Royal Enfield built the rarest of competitive advantages: emotional monopolisation.

Booking Holdings: A Platform Moat Powered by Network Effects

Booking.com thrives on a self-reinforcing flywheel: more listings attract more travellers, and more travellers bring in more listings. This two-sided network effect, enhanced by vast data and personalisation, has made it the default aggregator for hotels across Europe and beyond.

Its moat lies not only in inventory depth but also in the trust and convenience it delivers. Rich user reviews, superior search and discovery, and global demand aggregation lock in both travellers and properties. Hotel chains may try to push direct bookings, but few can match Booking's reach, conversion rates or optimisation algorithms. The result: a durable platform moat, where scale itself compounds into defensibility.

Bajaj Finance: Building a Fortress in Plain Sight

Bajaj Finance's moat rests on its ability to transform consumer lending into a data-rich ecosystem. Its proprietary underwriting models, disciplined risk management and technology integration have created durable competitive edges.

The company's EMI card, accepted across 170,000 merchants, functions as both a credit product and a lock-in mechanism, embedding Bajaj Finance into everyday retail commerce. By mastering segmentation and operationalising credit intelligence, Bajaj Finance turned consumer durable financing into a gateway for acquiring and retaining new-to-credit customers. Over time, this evolved into a fintech-like flywheel, where data, trust and repeat usage deepen customer stickiness. While rivals compete primarily on pricing, Bajaj Finance compounds on relationships and scale intelligence.

Moat Type Table with Expanded Companies

Moat Type	Example Companies
Brand Power	Titan, Monster, Kweichow Moutai, Eicher Motors
Proprietary Technology	Ansys, ASML
Network Effects	Amazon, Netflix, NVIDIA, Booking Holdings
High Switching Costs	Apple, Infosys, Microsoft
Operational Excellence	HDFC Bank, Home Depot, Walmart, Bajaj Finance
Data & Analytics	FICO, Netflix, Bajaj Finance
Cultural & Regulatory	Kweichow Moutai

Investor Takeaways

A large TAM gets you altitude; a strong moat keeps you there. Without defensibility, growth begets competition and profits erode as quickly as they rose. True moats are silent compounders; they whisper through expanding margins, enduring customer loyalty, and pricing power that holds even in downturns. Whether it's ASML's technological stranglehold, Titan's institutionalised trust, or Netflix's data-driven flywheel, moats are the safety ropes that turn early wins into decades of dominance.

CHAPTER

5 Pillar 3 - Reinvestment Power: Multiplying Growth, Not Preserving It

I try to stay ahead of things, if you know what I mean.
I take the money I make and reinvest it.

— ***Mickey Gilley***

Growth without reinvestment is fleeting. Companies that consistently redeploy profits into high-return opportunities build compounding flywheels, turning 10× stories into 100× legends. The art of reinvestment lies in allocating each dollar of free cash flow into initiatives that deepen moats, expand ecosystems or ignite new growth engines.

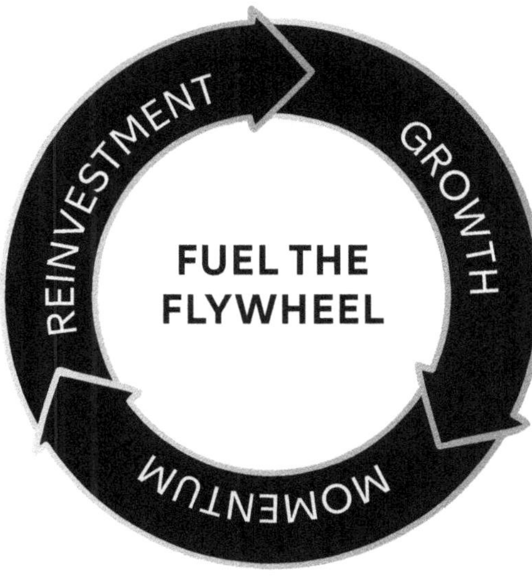

Strategic Reinvestment Flywheels

Microsoft: Reinvestment Flywheel in the Cloud Era

Microsoft's cloud era transformation hinged on pouring billions into Azure since 2008 and building a global network of hyperscale data centres and embedding the platform into enterprise workflows through developer tools, APIs and integrations.

A series of targeted acquisitions accelerated this flywheel: Xamarin (2016, US $400–500M) added cross-platform mobile tools; LinkedIn (2016, US $26.2B) fused professional networking with Microsoft's productivity stack; GitHub (2018, US $7.5B) secured developer mindshare; and Nuance (2021, US $19.7B) strengthened AI and industry-specific cloud capabilities.

Azure's growing adoption generated high-margin recurring revenues, funding further R&D in AI, security, and hybrid cloud solutions. By FY 2025, Azure and cloud services delivered over US$80 billion in revenue at ~47% operating margins, reinforced by cross-product synergies with Microsoft 365, Dynamics, LinkedIn, GitHub, and Nuance. The result: Microsoft evolved from a Windows-bound incumbent into the foundational operating layer of the modern digital economy.

Titan: The Reinvestment Flywheel

From ~40 stores in 2001 to 505 in 297+ Indian cities and 23 overseas outlets by March 2025, Titan has reinvested steadily in scale and capability. Profits have funded entry into tier-2 and tier-3 cities, upgraded existing showrooms, and expanded integrated manufacturing and karigar parks to guarantee purity and faster turnaround.

This reinvestment has extended beyond physical infrastructure into backend supply chain digitisation, design innovation and omnichannel platforms that blend in-store service with online convenience. The result is a growth loop: wider reach strengthens brand equity, which boosts margins, generating the cash flows that finance further expansion. Over two decades, this loop has turned Titan into a compounding machine.

Amazon: The Relentless Reinvestment Flywheel

Starting with razor-thin e-commerce margins, Amazon channelled nearly every dollar of cash flow into three reinforcing growth engines:

- Fulfilment & FBA – Building one of the largest logistics networks in history, enabling fast delivery and supporting millions of sellers.
- Prime Ecosystem – bundling shipping, deals, and entertainment to drive higher purchase frequency and lifetime value.
- AWS – Monetising Internal Cloud Expertise into the World's Most Profitable Cloud Business.

Strategic acquisitions, such as Whole Foods in 2017, extended reach into grocery. Heavy investment in AI, robotics, and last-mile delivery kept costs low and speed high. By 2024, AWS generated US $107 billion in revenue at ~37% operating margins, subsidising aggressive pricing, international expansion, and R&D. The compounding loop – Prime members driving sales, attracting sellers, improving selection, boosting economics, and funding further reinvestment – has powered two decades of exponential growth.

HDFC Bank Technology and Branch Reinvestment

HDFC Bank built its dominance not by choosing between branches and technology, but by reinvesting in both. While peers leaned heavily on physical expansion, HDFC Bank channelled profits into mobile and internet banking, advanced data analytics, and risk management systems, ensuring scale could grow without costs spiralling.

Reinvestment extended through targeted acquisitions. The 2000 purchase of Times Bank, India's first private sector bank merger, strengthened its metro presence and boosted deposits. The 2008 acquisition of Centurion Bank of Punjab added a nationwide branch footprint and diversified lending into SME and agriculture. Combined with steady organic branch rollout, these moves created a balanced retail and wholesale franchise. The outcome was faster loan approvals, lower cost-to-income ratios, and return on equity that consistently outpaced peers – a reinvestment flywheel that compounded growth into market leadership.

Apple: Reinvestment Flywheel in Innovation and Supply Chains

Apple's turnaround under Steve Jobs was anchored in aggressive reinvestment. In the early 2000s, Apple allocated ~8% of revenue to R&D, fuelling breakthroughs like the iPod, iTunes and iPhone. This commitment extended into custom chip development (A-series, later M-series), enabling performance and integration advantages rivals couldn't match.

Parallel investments in supply chains created resilience and efficiency. Apple committed billions to tooling for partners like Foxconn, precision assembly and logistics optimisation. The flywheel became self-reinforcing: design excellence and manufacturing scale supported premium pricing; high margins funded more R&D; and each cycle tightened the moat. Unlike many firms that returned cash to shareholders, Apple's reinvestment compounded its capabilities, turning profits into a perpetual innovation engine.

Kweichow Moutai: Capacity Discipline and Brand Heritage

Between 2003 and 2010, Moutai rose from a regional baijiu maker to China's ultimate prestige liquor brand. By consolidating distribution, rationing supply, and steadily raising prices, Moutai positioned itself as a national treasure. Aligning with state prestige, it became the drink of official banquets, elite business dealings, and political symbolism.

This was Moutai's "base camp" period, when it transformed scarcity into a moat, heritage into pricing power, and national identity into brand equity. By 2010, Moutai had secured cultural entrenchment and economic resilience, laying the foundation for decades of compounding growth. From here, it could climb to become one of the world's most valuable liquor companies, not just a spirits producer but a luxury asset class in its own right.

Infosys Reinvestment Power: Building Capabilities and Global Scale

Infosys reinvested early consulting cash flows into strengthening delivery and scaling talent. It built large training academies, proprietary automation tools, and knowledge management systems that institutionalised process excellence. Its investments in AI-driven platforms, cloud partnerships, and domain-specific solutions enabled higher-margin repeatable offerings.

Geographic expansion reinforced this reinvestment loop. By creating a 'right-shore' model, Infosys could flexibly deliver work from India, nearshore hubs or client sites, optimising cost and speed. This reinvestment strategy compounded into a self-sustaining advantage: better capabilities attracted larger deals, which generated cash flows to fund further innovation and expansion.

ASML: R&D Intensity and Strategic Bets

ASML's rise was powered by one of the most aggressive reinvestment strategies in the industrial world. Between 1996 and 2003, it poured 15 – 20% of sales into R&D, seeding breakthroughs in optics, nanofabrication software and EUV prototypes. Its boldest move was the 2001 acquisition of Silicon Valley Group (SVG), which expanded its US presence and provided critical wafer-handling and resist-coating technologies, tightening ties with American semiconductor giants.

This reinvestment philosophy, combining heavy organic R&D with targeted acquisitions, created a compounding loop: new breakthroughs reinforced ASML's dominance, which funded more research, which widened the moat further. Unlike peers who optimised for short-term margins, ASML doubled down on long-horizon bets, turning technological risk into durable industry leadership.

NVIDIA: Reinvestment Power: High Intensity R&D and Strategic Bets

Nvidia's transformation was powered by aggressive reinvestment. Between 2010 and 2016, it consistently devoted 25% – 29% of revenue to R&D, among the highest intensities in the tech sector. GPU profits financed CUDA development, deep-learning libraries and new architectures like Fermi, Kepler and Maxwell, which pushed GPUs into AI, HPC and data analytics.

Reinvestment also extended to the supply chain and partnerships. Nvidia secured wafer capacity with TSMC, advanced packaging technologies, and forged long-term alliances with hyperscalers, automotive OEMs, and research labs. This high - intensity cycle lifted operating margins from ~15% in 2016 to over 60% by 2025. By compounding reinvestment into hardware, software, and ecosystems, Nvidia turned technological foresight into exponential value creation.

AutoZone: Logistics, DIFM Services & Strategic Acquisitions

AutoZone's compounding story was fuelled by disciplined reinvestment into both physical assets and intangibles. The company poured capital into advanced inventory management systems, automated distribution centres, and DIFM services, which connected its retail base with professional mechanics. These reinvestments translated into higher same-store sales, better margins, and a stronger lock-in with customers.

Acquisitions amplified this reinvestment strategy:

- 1996: ALLDATA Corp. ($56.8M): Proprietary automotive diagnostics and repair software, strengthening ties with repair professionals.
- 1998: Chief Auto Parts (550+ stores), Auto Palace (112 stores), and TruckPro (43 outlets): Rapid geographic expansion and entry into heavy-duty trucks.
- 2013: AutoAnything.com: A leading e-commerce platform, extending AutoZone into online retail and omnichannel distribution.

Each acquisition was integrated into its logistics backbone, creating a self-reinforcing loop: greater distribution scale improved availability and speed, which attracted more professional accounts and retail customers, further funding innovation and expansion.

Netflix: Content & Technology Reinvestment Flywheel

Netflix's ascent was powered by relentless reinvestment into content, technology and global expansion. After launching streaming in

2007, the company initially relied on licensed titles, spending under $1 billion annually. By 2013, it doubled down on originals, pushing content spend to $2.4 billion, which rose to over $16 billion by 2024.

Strategic acquisitions amplified this content engine:

- Millarworld (2017): Secured comic book IP for future franchises.
- ABQ Studios (2018): Added proprietary production capacity.
- Scanline VFX (2021), Night School Studio (2021), Next Games (2022): Expanded into visual effects and interactive storytelling.

In parallel, billions were invested in the Open Connect CDN, AI-driven personalisation, and partnerships with device makers to embed Netflix directly into living room ecosystems. These reinvestments formed a flywheel where superior delivery and content reinforced subscriber growth, funding still more innovation — a compounding loop that defined Netflix's capital allocation philosophy.

Monster Beverage: Reinvesting in Culture & Distribution

Monster reinvested consistently in niche marketing, sponsoring extreme sports, music festivals and gaming to deepen loyalty with young consumers. Marketing spend consistently ran 12–15% of sales, creating brand equity that compounded over time. The Coca-Cola equity partnership in 2015 provided global bottling and logistics leverage, extending Monster's reach across continents. These reinvestments expanded operating margins from ~6% in 2002 to ~26% in 2024, proving that targeted reinvestment in brand and distribution can compound into both scale and profitability.

Home Depot: Stores, Supply Chains & Pro Services

Home Depot reinvested early profits into rapid store expansion, growing from 63 stores in 1985 to over 2,300 by 2024. Alongside this footprint growth, it built centralised distribution centres, cross-dock hubs, and IoT-enabled inventory systems, lifting efficiency and in-stock rates. Its Pro Services arm, dedicated desks, bulk delivery, and loyalty programmes ensured repeat engagement from contractors. By channelling profits back into infrastructure and customer solutions, Home Depot created a reinforcing loop of scale, service, and margin expansion.

Walmart: Technology, Omnichannel & Global Bets

Walmart's reinvestment flywheel has consistently focused on supply chain modernisation and technology. From pioneering satellite-linked inventory systems in the 1980s to robotics-driven warehouses today, reinvestment has kept Walmart structurally advantaged. Globally, reinvestment funded its expansion into Canada, Mexico, and Asia, capped by the $16 billion acquisition of Flipkart in 2018 to secure leadership in India's e-commerce market. These moves ensured Walmart's relevance not only in discount retail but also in the digital-first retail era.

Ansys: Strategic Acquisitions and Deep Workflow Integration

Ansys reinvested aggressively to expand its capabilities and entrench itself deeper in engineering workflows. Between 2000 and 2007, its acquisitions included ICEM CFD (2000), CFX (2003) for approximately $21 million, and Fluent Inc. (2006) for ~$565 million, extending its leadership in computational fluid dynamics and multiphysics simulation. These acquisitions, alongside continuous R&D in solvers, cloud-based licensing, and enterprise collaboration, allowed Ansys to become indispensable across industries. Every reinvested dollar reinforced its ecosystem lock-in: once companies standardised on Ansys, switching became economically and operationally prohibitive.

FICO: Reinforcement of Data & Analytics Platform via R&D, Institutional Integration and Strategic Acquisitions

FICO has sustained and expanded its dominance in credit scoring by consistently reinvesting in machine learning R&D, forging data partnerships, and building advanced compliance tools. Around 10% of revenues were allocated to R&D in fiscal 2024, reflecting a long-term commitment that dates back to the formative 2000–2007 period. These efforts embedded FICO scores deeply into the U.S. lending system, where banks, regulators, and credit bureaus standardised on its algorithms. The result was institutional lock-in: abandoning FICO risked disrupting the entire flow of consumer credit.

To reinforce this position, FICO pursued a series of targeted acquisitions that extended its analytics capabilities and broadened its global footprint. The purchase of HNC Software in 2002 enhanced fraud detection and predictive analytics, while Braun Consulting in 2004 strengthened its CRM and precision marketing. CR Software (2012) expanded its role in collections, Infoglide Software (2013) bolstered fraud prevention through entity resolution, and the 2018 acquisition of Brazil-based GoOn opened doors to Latin America's credit markets. Integrated with FICO's scoring and decision management systems, these moves created a platform characterised by high switching costs, global reach, and resilient margins, cementing its role as the operating system of consumer credit.

Royal Enfield: Reinvesting in Culture, Capacity, and Global Ambition

Royal Enfield's reinvestment strategy went beyond plants and products; it reinvested in culture. Early profits were ploughed into brand storytelling, riding communities, and rituals like 'One Ride', deepening its identity as the custodian of a global motorcycling culture. Customers became advocates, turning passion into grassroots marketing.

At the same time, Eicher Motors invested heavily in scaling operations. New plants at Oragadam and Vallam Vadagal brought modernised manufacturing while maintaining craftsmanship. A strengthened dealer network widened accessibility, and global expansion carried the brand into Europe, North America, and Latin America. Dedicated R&D in Chennai and London yielded models like the Interceptor 650, Meteor, and Himalayan, bikes that resonated with international riders while preserving the Enfield DNA. With industry-leading margins and strong free cash flows, reinvestment was disciplined and brand-consistent, elevating Royal Enfield from an Indian icon into a global phenomenon.

Booking Holdings: Precision Reinvestment, Maximum Compounding

Booking exemplifies disciplined reinvestment, deploying capital into adjacencies that expand its ecosystem while keeping the model asset light. The $133 million acquisition of Booking.com in 2005 became its global launchpad. In 2013, it added KAYAK to capture consumer intent earlier in the travel journey, and in 2018, FareHarbor extended reach into tours and activities, high-margin experiences that deepen engagement.

Internally, Booking has invested steadily in AI-driven personalisation, pricing algorithms, and mobile-first booking flows. These require modest capex but create enduring advantages in conversion and retention. By 2024, the company generated $7.9 billion in free cash flow and returned much of it to shareholders, repurchasing $1.8 billion of stock in Q1 2025, with $25.9 billion still authorised for buybacks.

This reinvestment model compounds in three ways: acquisitions expand TAM, technology sharpens execution, and free cash flow is recycled into shareholder returns. It is a textbook example of capital discipline and multiplying growth.

Bajaj Finance: Reinvesting for Exponential Growth

From an AUM of ₹2,478 crore in FY2008 to ₹4,032 crore in FY2010, and then soaring to ₹4.17 lakh crore by FY2025, Bajaj Finance has expanded at a pace few financial institutions can match. With consistently high return on equity (18–22%) and a diversified loan book, it has redeployed internal accruals into high-yield lending, customer acquisition, technology platforms and geographic expansion, without significant equity dilution.

This reinvestment has gone far beyond balance sheet growth. Digital onboarding, AI-driven underwriting and omnichannel service delivery have reinforced its cost advantage and customer loyalty. New verticals — personal loans, SME credit, home finance and wealth management — have multiplied its scale rather than preserved it. Every rupee earned has been channelled into widening the opportunity set, transforming linear growth into exponential value creation. In Terminal Value Investing terms, Bajaj Finance exemplifies the convergence of time, reinvestment and execution into compounding momentum.

Asset-Light Compounders vs. Capital-Heavy Builders

Not every 100× success story requires factories or gigawatts of capex. Asset-light models like Visa, Moody's, or Google Search generate massive cash flows with minimal incremental spend. Their reinvestment focus shifts to software, data, or ecosystem extensions, whilst surplus capital often flows into share buybacks or strategic partnerships.

Investor Takeaways

"Altitude and safety mean nothing if you stop climbing."

- Allocate Wisely: Reinvestment must target areas of sustainable high returns, whether it's next-generation technology (ASML), content intellectual property (Netflix), or distribution arms (Coca-Cola & Monster).
- Deepen the Moat: Use cash flows to reinforce competitive barriers, be that proprietary R&D (NVIDIA) or trust (Titan).
- Balance Heavy vs. Light: Recognise when to build assets (fulfilment centres, factories) and when to leverage asset-light scalability (software platforms, data networks).
- Return When Appropriate: If no reinvestment surpasses your cost of capital, returning cash via buybacks or dividends can compound per-share value.

Reinvestment – when intelligent compounds both growth and defensibility; when aimless, it merely bloats the balance sheet. Just as blueprints today become skyscrapers tomorrow, reinvestment turns current earnings into enduring foundations of power.

CHAPTER

6

Patience – The Fourth Pillar of Terminal Value Investing: The Unseen Force Driving Generational Wealth

The stock market is a device for transferring money from the impatient to the patient."

— ***Warren Buffett***

The rarest quality in investing is not insight, it is patience. Every great investment story hinges on time: the years (or decades) during which compounding works its quiet magic. Spotting the right business is essential, but the real challenge lies in holding it through storms, scepticism and market euphoria alike.

Patience is the Fourth Pillar of Terminal Value Investing because even the largest market, the deepest moat, and the strongest reinvestment engine are powerless without the holding period to let them work. It is the discipline that allows altitude to be reached, safety to hold, and oxygen to keep flowing long after the initial climb.

LET TIME DO THE HEAVY LIFTING.

Enduring the Storms: Titan's Two-Decade Ascent

In 2002, Rakesh Jhunjhunwala began accumulating Titan shares at approximately ₹2 (split- and bonus-adjusted). At that point, Titan was a promising watchmaker making a bold foray into India's unbranded gold jewellery market, an industry dominated by local family jewellers and rife with informal practices.

Over the next twenty-plus years, Titan weathered:

- Global shocks such as the 2008 financial crisis, when consumer sentiment froze and discretionary spending collapsed.
- Strategic pivots, balancing watches, jewellery and eyewear while stretching management bandwidth and capital.
- Regulatory headwinds, including import duties and hallmarking mandates that squeezed margins.

By 2025, Titan traded above ₹3,600, a staggering 1,800× gain. The secret wasn't perfect timing but the resolve to stay invested through every setback and pivot. Jhunjhunwala's conviction allowed the power of compounding, brand building and market expansion to play out over two decades.

Why Compounding Rewards the Patient

- The Rule of 72: At an annualised 25% return, wealth doubles roughly every three years.
- Early plateau vs. late explosion: A great business might triple in its first decade, but by the second, the same holding can be worth 80× or more. The magic happens late, when compounding accelerates.
- A psychological moat: patience itself becomes a defence mechanism, shielding investors from impulsive selling during volatility.

Cultivating Patience: An Active Discipline

Patience isn't passive waiting. It demands:

1. Deep conviction in your thesis – so you can resist noise and doubt.
2. A clear re-assessment framework - knowing when to double down or when the original thesis has broken.
3. Emotional self-control – overcoming fear during drawdowns and greed during bull runs.

The investor who survives the early turbulence often becomes the one best positioned to capture the most explosive phase of compounding.

Investor Takeaways: The Final Edge Few Possess

"Most investors sprint to the first camp. The great ones stay for the full climb."

- Resist the urge to harvest early – small wins can cost you the big prize.
- Embrace volatility – it's the admission price for exceptional returns.
- Align time horizons – match your investment horizon to the business's runway; moats and reinvestment cycles often take a decade or more to fully manifest.
- Review your thesis, not the ticker – focus on the story of the business, not the flicker of the screen.

Conclusion: Assembling Your Everest Toolkit

1. Market Size gives you the altitude, how high your investment can go.

2. Moats provide safety, ensuring competitors cannot erode your gains.
3. Reinvestment Power supplies oxygen, fuelling ongoing growth.
4. Patience carries you through the final, steepest ascent, when the climb is hardest and visibility lowest.

When these four pillars align, wealth creation shifts from speculation to inevitability. Patience doesn't just keep you in the game; it wins it.

In the next chapter, we'll lay out the complete framework of Terminal Value Investing, equipping you with the maths, metrics, and mindset to chart your own Everest of compounding. Later, in Chapter 17: The Patience Premium: Legendary Investors Who Let Time Do the Heavy Lifting, we will return to this theme, not as theory, but through the lived journeys of legendary investors like Warren Buffett, Tom Alberg, Nick Sleep, and others who proved that patience, coupled with quality, can deliver extraordinary long-term results.

CHAPTER

7

What is Terminal Value

"The value of any stock, bond, or business today is determined by the cash inflows and outflows discounted at an appropriate interest rate that can be expected to occur during the remaining life of the asset."

— John Burr Williams, The Theory of Investment Value (1938)

Before the Ascent: Mapping the Forecast Horizon

To understand Terminal Value, we must first understand the landscape of intrinsic valuation, which is the foundation upon which all value calculations are built. At its core, intrinsic value estimates a company's future cash flows and discounts them back to present value using an appropriate cost of capital. The most widely used method, the Discounted Cash Flow (DCF) model, breaks this journey into two main phases:

- **Forecast Period:** The explicit years where cash flows are projected year by year.
- **Terminal Period:** The period beyond the forecast horizon, where cash flows are assumed to grow at a stable, long-term rate.

Surprisingly, it's this Terminal Period and not the near-term projections that often accounts for the majority of a company's intrinsic value.

Defining Terminal Value

Terminal Value is the estimated present worth of all the cash flows a business is expected to generate beyond the explicit forecast period, under the assumption that the company will continue operating indefinitely. These cash flows are expected to grow at a steady rate into perpetuity and are discounted back using the company's Weighted Average Cost of Capital (WACC) expected during the Terminal Period.

In other words, Terminal Value captures the enduring value of a business after the detailed forecasts end, an essential component of the valuation puzzle, especially for long-lived firms.

How Do We Estimate Terminal Value?

There are two main methods:

1. Perpetuity Growth Method (Gordon Growth Model)
   This is the most rigorous way to model Terminal Value for stable, compounding businesses. It assumes that free cash flows will grow indefinitely at a modest, sustainable rate typically close to the long-term nominal GDP.

$$\text{Terminal Value} = \frac{\text{FCFT} \times (1 + g).}{(\text{WACC} - g)}$$

Present Value of Terminal Value is Terminal Value × Discount Factor in the Last Year of Forecast Period

Where:

- FCFT = Free cash flow in the final forecast year
- g = Terminal growth rate (realistic, stable growth into perpetuity)

- WACC = Weighted Average Cost of Capital
- DF is the Discount Factor for the last year of the Forecast Period.

2. Exit Multiple Method
   This approach applies a valuation multiple (like EV/EBITDA or P/E) to year-n earnings or cash flows and applies the discount factor in the last year of the Forecast Period. It is simpler, widely used by most investors but highly sensitive to market sentiment, often baking in valuation bubbles or pessimism from the current cycle.

Because Terminal Value condenses decades of performance into one number, even small changes in assumptions (g or WACC) can swing valuation dramatically. That's why terminal inputs must be grounded in macro context and company-specific durability.

Therefore, in our explanation we stick to the Perpetuity Growth Method.

Key Inputs That Drive Terminal Value

To accurately compute Terminal Value, we must understand the three core inputs that shape its magnitude:

1. Free Cash Flow in the Target Year (FCFT)
   This is the Free Cash Flow in the final year of the forecast period. It serves as the base level from which all future perpetual cash flows are projected. FCFT is calculated as:

FCFT = NOPAT − Net Capital Investments

- NOPAT: Operating Profit After Tax
- Net Capital Investments: Includes steady-state investments in fixed assets, including acquisitions and net working capital, required to support long-term growth and operations.

In analytical terms, FCFT can also be modelled using the following components:

- Sales and Growth Rates
- Operating Margin
- Tax Rate
- Incremental Investment Rate (Increment Capex / Incremental Sales) Plus (Incremental Net Working Capital / Incremental Sales)

These inputs collectively reflect the business's reinvestment needs and efficiency in turning operating profits into free cash flows.

2. Terminal Growth Rate (g)
   This is the assumed perpetual growth rate of cash flows beyond the forecast period. It typically reflects a blend of:
   - Inflationary growth: reflects the company's pricing power and ability to raise prices in line with long-term inflation.
   - Real growth: Accounts for long-term economic growth (country and world GDP growth), industry, and company-specific expansion.

There are three practical assumptions one can apply:

- Cash flows grow at inflation + real growth
- Cash flows grow at inflation alone
- Cash flows remain constant (zero growth)

A conservative estimate is often used to avoid overstating value. Importantly, the Terminal Growth Rate must always be less than the company's WACC, as growth beyond the cost of capital would imply infinite value.

1. Weighted Average Cost of Capital (WACC)
   WACC is the discount rate used to value both the forecast and terminal periods. It reflects the average return required by all providers of capital — debt and equity. During the terminal period, WACC should account for the company's long-term capital structure, inflation, risk-free rate, stability, and risk profile.

Terminal Value Explained: Walmart

Let's now bring the concept of terminal value to life using Walmart as an example.

Walmart generates approximately $20 billion for the year 2024 in Free Cash Flow and is expected to grow in perpetuity at 4.5% comprised of 2.5% inflation and 2% real growth. Its Weighted Average Cost of Capital (WACC) is assumed to be 8.17%.

Key Assumptions:

Metric	Value
Current FCFF	$20 billion
Year 1 Growth	5%
Year 1 FCFF	$21 billion
Terminal Growth Rate (g)	4.5%
WACC	8.17%
Discount Factor (Year 1)	0.924
Present Value of Terminal Value	$552 billion

Terminal Value Calculation

We first compute the Terminal Value at the end of Year 1 using the Perpetuity Growth Method:

TV = FCFT (Year1) × (1+g) / (WACC−g)
= $21 × (1.045) / (8.17% – 4.5%) = $598 billion

We then discount this Terminal Value back to the present using the Year 1 discount factor:

PV of {TV} = \$598 × 0.924 = \$552 billion

Terminal Growth Assumption Justification:

- U.S. real GDP growth: ~2%
- World GDP growth: ~3%
- Long-term U.S. inflation: ~2.5% over the past 30 years

Thus, a 4.5% terminal growth rate is a reasonable estimate, reflecting both inflation and modest real growth.

Terminal Value Explained – Tata Consultancy Services (TCS)

To further illustrate the concept of Terminal Value, let's apply it to Tata Consultancy Services (TCS), a leading Indian IT services company.

For the year ending March 2025, TCS generated approximately INR 450 billion in Free Cash Flow to the Firm (FCFF). We assume this cash flow will grow perpetually at 6%, comprising 4% inflation (primarily due to currency depreciation) and 2% real growth in the global IT services industry over the long term. The Weighted Average Cost of Capital (WACC) is assumed to be 9.22%.

Key Assumptions

Metric	Value
Current FCFF	₹450 billion
Year 1 Growth	5%
Year 1 FCFF	₹472 billion
Terminal Growth Rate (g)	6%
WACC	9.22%
Discount Factor (Year 1)	0.915
Present Value of Terminal Value	₹14,232 billion

Terminal Value Calculation

Using the Perpetuity Growth Method, Terminal Value (TV) at the end of Year 1 is calculated as:

TV = FCFF (Year1) × (1+g) / (WACC−g)
TV = 472 × (1.06) / (0.0922−0.06) = ₹15,538 billion

We then discount this Terminal Value back to the present:

PV of TV = 15,538 × 0.915 = ₹14,217 billion

Terminal Growth Assumption Justification

- Long-term real growth in global IT services: ~2%
- Long-term inflation in India: ~4%

Combining these gives us a reasonable 6% terminal growth rate, representing sustained industry relevance and currency-driven inflation over the long term.

Comparing Terminal Value Drivers: Walmart vs TCS

While both Walmart and Tata Consultancy Services (TCS) generate substantial free cash flows and have strong business fundamentals, their terminal values diverge due to key macroeconomic and market- and industry-specific variables. Below are the three main drivers behind this difference:

1. **Terminal Growth Rate**
   - Inflation Dynamics: India's long-term inflation is higher (~4%) compared to the US (~2.5%). This difference, often reflected in exchange rate trends, inflates nominal growth assumptions for Indian companies.

- Real Growth Expectations:
    - o TCS benefits from long-term global IT services industry growth (~2% real growth), supporting a 6% terminal growth estimate, which includes inflation reflected through exchange rate differences.
    - o Walmart, on the other hand, is tied more closely to U.S. and global GDP growth, estimated at a lower long-term pace (~2% real growth), resulting in a ~4.5% terminal growth rate.

2. **Cost of Capital (WACC)**
    - Higher Risk Premiums in Emerging Markets:
        - o TCS has a WACC of 9.22%, reflecting India's higher inflation, currency risk and equity risk premium.
        - o Walmart benefits from a lower-risk US environment, with a WACC of 8.17%.
    - Implication: Although TCS enjoys higher expected growth, the higher WACC partly neutralises its advantage in terminal value.
3. **Discounting Future Cash Flows**
    - Even a 1-year discounting period at 8–9% WACC levels has a significant impact on the present value of terminal values, especially when the future cash flows involved are in trillions or billions.
    - The discount factor is crucial when projecting long-dated cash flows and should never be overlooked.

Investor Insight: Terminal Value Reflects More Than Just Fundamentals

Terminal Value doesn't merely reward near-term profitability or cash flows; it accounts for:

- Macro environment
- Long-term inflation expectations

- Sustainable real growth
- Capital risk and required returns

The Importance of Geographic Context

- For Indian Companies: A terminal growth rate of around 7% may be reasonable for India-focused businesses. India's real GDP is currently growing at 6.5%, with inflation averaging around 4%, implying a 10.5% nominal growth rate. Over the long term, India's growth is expected to gradually converge with global GDP growth, making a 7% terminal growth assumption both realistic and defensible.
- For Mature U.S. Companies: Applying such high growth assumptions would be overly optimistic. Given the lower inflation and modest long-term real GDP growth in the U.S. and globally, a more conservative terminal growth rate of 4.5% is generally more appropriate.

Key Warning: Terminal Value Sensitivity

Terminal Value is highly sensitive to both the growth rate (g) and WACC. A mere 0.5% change in either can result in massive swings in valuation. Thus, one should use conservative, well-justified, geography and industry-specific assumptions when applying the Terminal Value formula.

Transitioning to Terminal Value Investing

The comparison between Walmart and TCS reveals a powerful insight: terminal value is not just a formulaic result; it is a lens through which we evaluate long-term business durability, shaped by macroeconomic realities, geographic nuance, and structural growth potential. Understanding how inflation, real growth, and capital costs vary across regions is essential for building conviction in any long-term valuation.

With this foundation in place, we now move into the heart of Terminal Value Investing, not merely as a theoretical idea, but as a hands-on framework. In the next chapter, we will apply this approach through a detailed hypothetical case study, using both a 5-year and a 20-year detailed cash flow forecast to illustrate the power and nuance of terminal value modelling. This dual-scenario analysis will help crystallise the concept and offer practical insights into identifying businesses with extraordinary compounding potential.

It's time to shift from theory to application and uncover how enduring value is truly built.

Investor Takeaways

Most of a company's value isn't in the next five years; it's in the decades that follow.

It's the value of the business's 'long tail' – all the profits it can keep generating once the initial forecast period ends. In other words:

It's the valuation of the company's forever.

CHAPTER

8

What is Terminal Value Investing

"If everything you do needs to work on a three-year time horizon, then you're competing against a lot of people. But if you're willing to invest on a seven-year time horizon, you're now competing against a fraction of those people… Just by lengthening the time horizon, you can engage in endeavours that you could never otherwise pursue."

— ***Jeff Bezos***

Introduction: The Summit Beyond the Forecast

Most investors stop climbing just as the real ascent begins. After the initial 5 or 10 years of forecasting, they pack up their models, missing the most powerful stretch of compounding. Terminal Value Investing is about looking beyond that artificial horizon, extending your vision into the decades where wealth is truly built.

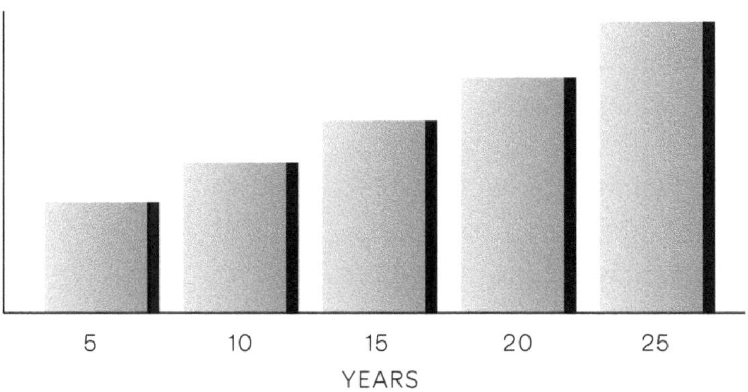

GREATNESS UNFOLDS IN THE DECADES NO ONE MODELS.

Traditional financial models often forecast 2, 5, or 10 years of cash flows, then abruptly cut off. Such shortcuts ignore the very nature of exceptional businesses: their ability to grow free cash flows and reinvest wisely over decades, not just years.

But let's be clear: Terminal Value is not a substitute for forecasting, it's the culmination of it. The real shareholder value is created during the forecast period, when companies widen moats, improve margins, and scale with discipline. A strong Terminal Value doesn't come from plugging in a hopeful multiple – it emerges by design, built on the foundation of a robust forecast.

Think of the forecast period as the climb, and the Terminal Value as the peak, the payoff for enduring the journey. Stopping at Year 10 in your model is like halting halfway up Everest and declaring victory. The real summit lies ahead, hidden from short-term sight but visible to those with long-term conviction.

Terminal Value Investing isn't just a modelling exercise; it's a belief system rooted in strategic endurance. While it shows up as a line item in a DCF model, its real meaning is revealed only when preceded by thoughtful, full-horizon forecasting.

To invest with terminal value in mind is to back companies that can actually deliver across time. It is not about projecting Year 6 to Year 30 for the sake of completeness; it is about identifying businesses with:

- Moats that deepen over time
- Margins that expand with scale
- Leaders who reinvest with discipline
- A Total Addressable Market (TAM) that keeps compounding

Where most investors seek quick wins, Terminal Value Investors seek compounding machines, businesses that reveal their greatness only with time. You're not betting on next quarter's earnings, you're investing in the next two decades of resilience and reinvestment.

In this philosophy, patience isn't passive, it's an active edge. The greatest returns often show up long after the crowd has moved on. Terminal Value Investing is how we position ourselves to be there when they do.

Mini Case: Buffett, Coca-Cola, and the Long View

Buffett's Coca-Cola purchase is the cleanest proof that terminal value can dominate intrinsic value. When Berkshire began buying in 1988, many models called KO 'expensive' on near-term multiples; Buffett looked past the next few years to the brand's global pricing power, habitual consumption, and decades of steady cash generation. In long-duration DCFs, most of the value sits beyond the first decade, and Coke's resilience across countries, channels, and cycles lets those far-future cash flows actually arrive. Rather than forecasting quarterly beats, Buffett underwrote durability: a franchise that could raise prices pennies at a time, defend margins with distribution and brand, and remit rivers of cash for decades (see Chapter 20 for figures).

Buffett wasn't just holding a stock. He was climbing the Everest of Terminal Value.

What Drives Terminal Value?

Driver	Why It Matters
ROIC	High returns on capital compound faster
TAM	Larger markets support longer growth runways
Moat Durability	Keeps competitors at bay for decades
Capital Allocation	Ensures profits are redeployed intelligently
Cost of Capital	Lower WACC boosts value of future cash

Terminal Value vs. Terminal Value Investing

Terminal Value is a DCF output.
Terminal Value Investing is a mindset.

You aren't just modelling beyond Year 5 — you're betting on moat endurance, margin expansion, TAM expansion, and reinvestment discipline over 10, 20, or even 30 years.

Let us now see this in action through a simple example and through the lens of an investor who saw the decades ahead, not just the quarters.

Deep Dive: The BlackRock Technologies Valuation Divide

Let's imagine a hypothetical company called BlackRock Technologies. Two investors analyse the same business, but with dramatically different time horizons.

Investor A builds a traditional 5-year DCF model. They observe that margins are gradually improving but end the forecast at Year 5, assigning a terminal value based largely on near-term assumptions. Their conclusion? The intrinsic value per share is approximately \$96, while the current market price is \$120—suggesting the stock is overvalued. Based on the projected cash flows and conservative terminal assumptions, the expected future value per share at the end of the 5th year is \$147, implying a modest IRR of 2.8%.

Investor B, in contrast, takes a long-term view. The investor extends the forecast to 20 years, modelling the compounding effect of steady margin expansion, consistently high ROIC, and disciplined reinvestment. With this broader horizon, they estimate the intrinsic value at \$1,315 per share, and a future value per share at the end of the 20th year at $7,368, translating into an attractive IRR of 22.4%.

The difference? Not in the Year 1 revenue or the P/E multiple but in the vision to see value beyond Year 5. Investor A modelled earnings. Investor B modelled endurance. Where one saw a plateau, the other saw a climb.

Compounding needs time to reveal its full power. A 5-year view might capture the narrative. A 20-year view can capture the legend.

Table Reference: Full Forecast Model for BlackRock Technologies

For a deeper understanding of Terminal Value Investing, detailed 5-year and 20-year financial forecasts for BlackRock Technologies have been included in Table 3 and Table 4. These models cover key metrics including projected sales, operating profit, tax outflows, capital investments, discount factors, the present value of cash flows and the computed present value of terminal value. Additionally, the models estimate future shareholder value under each scenario, illustrating how time horizon and compounding assumptions impact intrinsic valuation.

The Terminal Value Checklist

Risk/Insight	What to Look For
Overestimating Moats	Ensure moats are defensible, not just visible
Shrinking TAM	Make sure the market is expanding
Flawed Reinvestment	ROIC must remain above cost of capital
Poor Capital Discipline	Avoid stories that chase hype

Investor Takeaways – The Summit Is Far

Terminal Value is not a gimmick; it's the north star of long-term investing. When you climb the Everest of investing, the first few years are just base camp.

The real rewards lie higher up, where the fog clears and enduring businesses dominate.

Modelling those years faithfully is how investors stop selling too soon and start owning greatness.

Table 3: 5-Year Forecast & Terminal Value

Figure in $ / Million

Year	Sales	Sales Growth	OPM	Operating Profit	Tax 25%	Incremental Investments	NCF	Discount Factor @9%	PV of NCF
Prior	1000								
1	1500	50%	0%	0	0	150	-150	0.917	-137.6
2	2175	45%	5%	108.8	27	203	-121	0.842	-101.8
3	3045	40%	10%	304.5	76	261	-33	0.772	-25.2
4	4111	35%	12%	493.3	123	320	50	0.708	35.6
5	5344	30%	13%	694.7	174	370	151	0.650	98.2

Present Value of Cash flows	-131
Present Value of Terminal Value	2042
Shareholder Value	1911
Outstanding shares	20
Shareholder Value Per Share	96
Market Price	120
Future Value Per share at end of 5th Year	147.0
IRR	2.8%

Table 4: 20 Year Forecast & Terminal Value

Figure in $ / Million

Year	Sales	Sales Growth	OPM	Operating Profit	Tax 25%	Incremental Investments	NCF	Discount Factor @9%	PV of NCF
Prior	1000								
1	1500	50%	0%	0	0	150	-150	0.917	-137.6
2	2175	45%	5%	108.8	27	203	-121	0.842	-101.8
3	3045	40%	10%	304.5	76	261	-33	0.772	-25.2
4	4111	35%	12%	493.3	123	320	50	0.708	35.6
5	5344	30%	13%	694.7	174	370	151	0.650	98.2
6	6306	25%	13.50%	851	213	289	350	0.5908	206.7
7	7441	25%	14.00%	1042	260	341	441	0.5371	236.8
8	8780	25%	15.00%	1317	329	402	586	0.4883	286.1
9	10361	25%	16.00%	1658	414	474	769	0.4439	341.4
10	12226	25%	17.00%	2078	520	559	999	0.4036	403.3
11	14182	20%	17.50%	2482	620	587	1275	0.3669	467.6
12	16451	20%	18.00%	2961	740	681	1540	0.3335	513.7
13	19083	20%	18.50%	3530	883	790	1858	0.3032	563.4
14	22136	20%	19.00%	4206	1051	916	2238	0.2756	617.0
15	25678	20%	18.50%	4750	1188	1063	2500	0.2506	626.5
16	29273	15%	20.00%	5855	1464	1078	3312	0.2278	754.6
17	33371	15%	20.00%	6674	1669	1229	3776	0.2071	782.0
18	38043	15%	20.00%	7609	1902	1402	4305	0.1883	810.5
19	43369	15%	20.00%	8674	2168	1598	4908	0.1711	839.9
20	49441	15%	20.00%	9888	2472	1822	5595	0.1556	870.5

Present Value of Cash flows	8189
Present Value of Terminal Value	18106
Shareholder Value	26295
Outstanding shares	20

Shareholder Value Per Share	1315
Market Price	120
Future Value Per share at end of 20th Year	7368.0
IRR	22.4%

CHAPTER

9 Base Camp - The First Step to 100x

"The best way to predict the future is to create it."

— ***Peter Drucker***

Every extraordinary investing journey begins quietly. No ringing bells, no viral headlines, just a company with a modest but growing foothold, a product loved by a devoted niche, early signs of disciplined reinvestment, and a vast opportunity still ahead. The market barely notices. Yet it's in these understated beginnings that the seeds of generational returns are sown.

THE FIRST STEP TO 100×

In the Everest of Investing, Base Camp isn't about being the first to plant your flag. It's about recognising a business at a critical inflection point – when product market fit meets scalable reinvestment in the shadow of a vast Total Addressable Market (TAM). Most investors overlook it. Those who spot it, and have the patience to hold, can capture the decades-long compounding that transforms good businesses into 100x legends.

What Is Base Camp?

Base Camp marks the first true compounding stage of a company's life.
It's not a speculative pre-revenue dream.
It's not a mature cash cow milking its market.

It's the moment when a company:

- Has proven product-market fit.
- Is deliberately reinvesting into moats rather than maximising short-term profits.
- Faces a vast or expanding TAM.
- Remains misunderstood or undervalued by the market.

At Base Camp, conviction must outlast volatility.

Most businesses never get here; they stall in the foothills due to subscale execution, limited TAM, or fragile economics. But the rare few that do offer investors a singular opportunity: to ride two or three decades of compounding and extraordinary stock returns.

Characteristics of Base Camp Businesses

- Clear Product-Market Fit: Strong retention, rising engagement, and proven unit economics.

- Large or Expanding TAM: New geographies, adjacent categories, or formalisation of fragmented demand.
- Early Reinvestment Discipline: Capital flows into R&D, supply chains, brands, or platforms and not short-term margins.
- Market Scepticism: Often dismissed as 'too expensive', 'low margin', 'unscalable' or 'overhyped'.
- Founder-Led Conviction: High insider ownership, long-term vision, and mission-driven leadership.

Recognizing the Quiet Giants

Before a company becomes a household name or a 100x stock, it passes through a strategic window where fundamentals are solid but the market has yet to take notice. This is Base Camp: the stage where product-market fit is proven, revenues are climbing, and a defendable moat is in place, yet valuations remain grounded.

For investors, Base Camp is the sweet spot. Growth runways are long, competition is still mobilising, and management is quietly fortifying the business for the climb ahead. In these overlooked years, great companies reinvest patiently, forge partnerships, and deepen their competitive edge.

In this chapter, we revisit the Base Camp years of 19 remarkable businesses, moments when they were still misunderstood, but already laying the foundations for decades of compounding. Their journeys are told through narrative case studies, supported by Field Guide tables that distil their Base Camp timelines, TAM expansions, and moats.

Betting on New Frontiers

Some companies use their Base Camp years to venture into entirely new markets, making bold moves before the world sees their potential.

Microsoft (2008–2016): From Desktop Giant to Cloud Architect

Between 2008 and 2014, Microsoft stood at a strategic inflection point. PC sales were flattening, the mobile wave had crested without it, and its traditional desktop software dominance was under siege. The turning point arrived in 2014, when Satya Nadella became CEO and reoriented the company with a clear "cloud-first, mobile-first" mandate. Commencement and launch of Azure.

Under this vision, Microsoft poured billions into Azure, scaling a global network of data centres and building deep integrations with developers, enterprises, and even long-time rivals like SAP and Oracle. Strategic acquisitions powered the shift: Xamarin (2016) brought mobile developer tools into the fold, while LinkedIn (2016) fused professional networking with Microsoft's productivity and cloud ecosystem, expanding distribution and creating new monetisation loops.

This was Microsoft's "base camp" because it was the period where it rewired its business model, technology stack and partnerships to compete in, and ultimately help shape the emerging cloud and AI economy. By the end of this phase, Microsoft had shed its image as a Windows-bound incumbent and positioned itself as a central architect of a $2 trillion-plus digital infrastructure market, ready for the next leg of compounding growth.

Apple (2001–2008): From iPod to iPhone: Building the Ecosystem

Between 2001 and 2008, Apple staged one of the most remarkable comebacks in corporate history, laying the foundation for its eventual dominance. The iPod, launched in 2001, and the iTunes Store in 2003 reshaped how music was consumed, locking millions of users into Apple's emerging ecosystem. At the same time, the rollout of Apple Stores redefined retail, transforming stores into immersive brand experiences rather than transactional outlets. Apple was no longer just selling products; it was cultivating loyalty through a seamless blend of hardware, software and services.

Operationally, Apple mastered vertical integration, controlling the entire stack from design to distribution. iPod sales surged past 22.5 million units in fiscal 2004–05 and stayed above 20 million annually for eight consecutive years, peaking at nearly 55 million units in 2007–08. This torrent of cash fuelled R&D enabled investments in custom silicon and financed bold product bets. The Intel processor transition in 2006 revived the Mac, showcasing Apple's ability to adapt at scale. But the true inflection point came in 2007 with the iPhone, a convergence of phone, iPod and internet communicator. By 2008, with the App Store live, Apple had secured the ecosystem, credibility and momentum that would power its Everest ascent.

NVIDIA (2010–2016): From Gaming Champ to AI Infrastructure Kingmaker

Between 2010 and 2016, Nvidia pivoted from gaming chips to programmable engines for parallel computing. CUDA, nurtured through universities and research labs, became the go-to framework for training advanced algorithms, ensuring AI developers worked on Nvidia hardware.

At the same time, Nvidia invested in data centre grade GPUs, aligning with researchers, enterprises, and hyperscalers before the AI boom fully arrived. This period was Nvidia's "base camp" when it consolidated technical leadership, developer loyalty, and market credibility. Like climbers preparing for the summit, Nvidia fortified its foundations, positioning itself as the indispensable supplier of AI infrastructure when global demand for compute exploded.

ASML: Betting the Future on EUV

From 1996 to 2003, ASML embarked on one of the boldest climbs in semiconductor history: committing billions to EUV R&D when commercialisation was a decade away and success uncertain. Sceptics doubted whether EUV could ever work at scale. But ASML recognised that the continuation of Moore's Law required a radical breakthrough in lithography.

Strategic partnerships with Intel, TSMC, and Samsung not only injected vital funding but validated ASML's vision, forging a co-development ecosystem committed to EUV's success. By mastering the most complex stage of chipmaking, ASML secured its place as the indispensable enabler of advanced semiconductors. These were its 'Base Camp' years, the period when it built the technological foundation, commercial credibility, and ecosystem trust that would propel it to an unassailable monopoly and a central role in the multi-trillion-dollar global tech economy.

Field Guide: Betting on New Frontiers

Company	Base Camp Phase	TAM	Moat
Microsoft	2008–2016: Azure and cloud infrastructure push	Cloud & AI Services	Developer ecosystem + distribution
Nvidia	2010–2016: Gaming GPUs to AI computing	AI Infrastructure	Tech leadership + developer ecosystem
ASML	1996–2002: EUV R&D scale-up	Semiconductor Equipment	IP monopoly + TSMC lock-in
Apple	2001–2008: iPod to iPhone, retail + App Store	Mobile Devices & Services	Integrated HW–SW–services + brand + retail distribution

Formalizing and Modernizing Markets

In emerging markets, Base Camp is often about taking a fragmented, informal industry and giving it structure, trust and scale.

Titan: Building the Gold Standard (2001-2008)

Between 2001 and 2008, Titan Industries laid the foundation for what would become one of India's greatest retail transformations. The gold jewellery market was still overwhelmingly unorganised, dominated by family-run stores with opaque pricing and variable purity. Backed by Tata's credibility, Titan used its Tanishq brand to introduce a vertically integrated model combining in-house design, precision manufacturing, and a tightly managed retail network.

The store count nearly doubled in this period, from about 53 in FY2001 to 105 by FY2008, reaching beyond metros into tier-2 and tier-3 cities. Air-conditioned, standardised showrooms replaced haggling with transparent carat-based pricing, purity certification, and gold exchange programmes that reinforced trust. This period was Titan's base camp, the years when credibility, brand identity, and national scale were built, giving the company the strength and positioning to lead India's multi-billion-dollar shift from informal to organised jewellery retail.

HDFC Bank (2000-2008): Building the Retail Backbone

Between 2000 and 2008, HDFC Bank embedded itself into India's emerging middle class. It expanded into semi-urban and urban centres, launched tailored credit products for housing, personal and SME needs, and built a data-driven underwriting model that balanced rapid growth with asset quality.

Two strategic acquisitions marked this base camp phase: Times Bank in 2000, which expanded its branch network and deposit base, and Centurion Bank of Punjab in 2008, which added agricultural lending, SME strength, and deeper regional coverage. Partnerships with retailers, corporates, and government payment systems reinforced its presence, whilst early investments in digital banking positioned it for scale. These formative years created the credibility, trust, and infrastructure that powered HDFC Bank's ascent to a 100x compounder.

Bajaj Finance (2008–2013): Building the Retail Credit Flywheel

After the demerger of Bajaj Auto's financial services arm in 2008, Sanjiv Bajaj assumed leadership of Bajaj Finserv and reimagined Bajaj Finance's future. The company pivoted from its niche two-wheeler financing base into broader consumer and SME lending, pioneering point-of-sale financing with electronics retailers and consumer durable brands. This innovation embedded Bajaj Finance directly at the retail counter, making credit a seamless part of the buying decision.

During this phase, Bajaj Finance built its credit intelligence backbone. It applied advanced analytics, tailored scoring for thin-file customers, and disciplined collections to achieve rapid growth without compromising asset quality. SME lending was layered on the same model, extending its footprint into business credit. These years were Bajaj Finance's *base camp*: the period when it constructed its retail lending flywheel, anchored in brand trust, data-driven underwriting, and distribution partnerships that would power its dominance in the decades ahead.

Kweichow Moutai (2003–2010): Turning a Regional Spirit into a National Prestige Symbol

Between 2003 and 2010, Kweichow Moutai rose from a regional baijiu maker to China's ultimate prestige liquor brand. By consolidating distribution, tightly controlling supply and preserving scarcity, it steadily increased prices and reinforced its status as a luxury symbol. Aligning with state prestige, Moutai became the drink of official banquets and elite gifting, embedding itself in China's socio-political culture.

This was Moutai's Base Camp, the period when it built an unassailable moat of heritage, political symbolism and disciplined supply control. By decade's end, it had achieved cultural entrenchment and economic resilience, laying the foundation for decades of compounding growth as one of the world's most valuable liquor companies.

Field Guide: Formalising and Modernising Markets

Company	Base Camp Phase	TAM	Moat
Titan	2001–2008: Modernizing Indian jewellery	Gold Jewellery	Brand Trust + Retail Scale
HDFC Bank	2000–2008: Formalizing Indian retail banking	Retail Financial Services	Underwriting + Branch Scale
Bajaj Finance	2008–2013: Consumer Finance and SME lending ramp-up	Indian Retail Credit (~₹22 lakh Cr)	Risk Analytics + Operational Excellence + Data
Kweichow Moutai	2003–2010: Brand formalization + channel control	Premium Alcohol (Baijiu)	Cultural Prestige + State Moat

Base Camps of Global Standards: From Software Delivery to Simulation to Credit Infrastructure

Infosys Base Camp (1994–1998): Establishing the Global Delivery Standard

Between 1994 and 1998, Infosys laid the foundations of its long-term compounding journey. Riding the surge in Y2K remediation demand, it secured long-term outsourcing contracts while perfecting its offshore delivery model. By blending low-cost, high-quality Indian engineering talent with on-site client coordination, Infosys delivered consistent outcomes at scale.

Backed by SEI-CMM Level 5 certifications, it became the benchmark for quality in global software services. This period was Infosys's "Base Camp" – when it established operational credibility, delivery discipline, and brand trust. The global delivery model built then became the cornerstone of Infosys's ascent, enabling later moves into consulting, digital transformation, and large-scale managed services.

Ansys (2000–2007): Building the Infrastructure of Modern Design

The early 2000s marked Ansys's 'Base Camp' years, when it transitioned from niche simulation vendor to industry standard. Through key acquisitions like Fluent and CFX, Ansys integrated advanced multiphysics and fluid dynamics into its portfolio, embedding simulation into the DNA of aerospace, automotive, and industrial design. These years created the foundation for its growth: engineers across industries standardised on Ansys, locking in decades of recurring use and compounding growth potential.

FICO (2000–2007): Becoming the Operating System of Credit

Between 2000 and 2007, FICO evolved from a scoring provider into the embedded operating system of US consumer credit. By becoming mandatory in mortgage, auto, and credit card approvals, FICO scores became institutionalised across banks, regulators, and bureaus. At the same time, investments in analytics platforms ensured that its algorithms sat at the heart of credit decision-making.

This was FICO's Base Camp: the years when it secured its position as indispensable infrastructure for global lending, laying the groundwork for decades of compounding.

Field Guide – Turning Technology into Global Standards

Company	Base Camp Phase	TAM	Moat
Infosys	1994–1998: Y2K tailwinds and outsourcing	Global IT Services	Talent + Process Trust
Ansys	2000–2007: Engineering simulation scaling	Simulation Software	IP + Switching Costs
FICO	2000–2007: Embedded credit scoring	Financial Analytics	Embedded Standards

Pivoting Before the World Believed

Amazon (2001–2009): Building the Flywheel Before the World Believed

Emerging from the dot-com crash, Amazon spent much of the 2000s in heavy reinvestment mode, laying the foundation for its future dominance. It expanded from books into electronics, apparel, home goods and a growing third-party marketplace, each addition strengthening the "customer flywheel."

A turning point came in 2005 with the launch of Amazon Prime, transforming casual shoppers into loyal members and boosting order frequency. In 2006, AWS debuted almost as an internal experiment, offering pay-as-you-go cloud services that would become Amazon's profit engine. By the end of the decade, Prime, logistics scale, and AWS were in place, critical infrastructure that competitors could neither match quickly nor cheaply. This was Amazon's base camp: a period of thin margins, external scepticism, and relentless capability-building that set the stage for the 100x ascent.

Netflix: 2002–2010: Laying the Tracks for Streaming Supremacy

Between 2002 and 2010, Netflix made its boldest bet: transitioning from DVDs to streaming before the market was ready. In 2007, it quietly launched 'Watch Now', offering just 1,000 online titles, barely 1% of its physical catalogue. Investors doubted the model, margins were thin, and streaming infrastructure was untested.

Yet Netflix methodically built the foundations. It forged licensing deals, partnered with device makers like Roku and Sony to make streaming the 'default button' in living rooms, and scaled its content delivery systems for seamless viewing. By embedding its brand across platforms and daily habits, Netflix established credibility and consumer loyalty during years when streaming was still a niche experiment. These base camp years, when scepticism was highest, laid the operational and technological tracks for its ascent to global dominance.

Monster Beverage: 1998–2008: Building the Lifestyle Engine

Between 1998 and 2008, Monster Energy rose from a challenger in the crowded beverage market to a dominant cultural symbol. Rooted in extreme sports - motocross, skateboarding, snowboarding – and later expanding into music festivals and gaming, Monster built a lifestyle brand around energy, rebellion and performance.

A turning point came in the mid-2000s with its partnership with Coca-Cola's bottling and distribution network, granting instant global reach and shelf space competitors couldn't match. By decade's end, Monster had fused brand equity with distribution dominance, making every can both a product and a statement.

This decade was Monster's base camp, the period that set the pillars of its compounding engine: a differentiated lifestyle brand, deep consumer loyalty and global distribution infrastructure, paving the way for sustained revenue and margin growth.

Field Guide: Pivoting Before the World Believed

Company	Base Camp Phase	TAM	Moat
Amazon	2001–2009: E-commerce flywheel to AWS	Retail + Cloud Infrastructure	Logistics + Platform
Netflix	2002–2010: DVDs to streaming pivot	Global Media	Content + Data + Habit
Monster	1998–2008: Energy branding and channel scale	Functional Beverages	Brand + Distribution

Scaling Physical Moats

Home Depot: 1985–1990: Scaling the Warehouse Model and Cementing Loyalty

Between 1985 and 1990, Home Depot expanded from 63 to 145 stores, targeting high-growth housing markets. These weren't just stores; they were proof of concept for a scalable warehouse format. Simultaneously, Home Depot invested in centralised distribution, favourable vendor contracts and inventory precision. These five years, when it scaled quietly but deliberately, were its Base Camp: the period where scale, efficiency and contractor loyalty were forged.

Walmart: 1975–1985: Engineering the Everyday-Low-Price Machine

From 1975 to 1985, Walmart evolved from a regional discounter into a formidable national player by perfecting its everyday-low-price strategy. In 1975, the company operated *125 stores* across five states. By 1985, the store count had grown to *882 locations* nationwide, reflecting a decade of relentless expansion.

This transformation was powered by two critical innovations:

- Exclusive supplier partnerships and scale-driven purchasing, which reinforced Walmart's ability to undercut competitors on price.
- The pioneering use of a satellite-linked inventory management system, enabling real-time stock tracking and faster replenishment across its growing network.

Though less visible to the casual shopper than later brand milestones, these operational advances formed Walmart's Base Camp, a logistical and pricing fortress that supported its climb to retail dominance in the decades ahead.

AutoZone (1995–2001): Building the Distribution Moat

Between 1995 and 2001, AutoZone constructed the foundation for its long-term growth. The company developed its hub-and-spoke distribution network, enabling rapid parts delivery and unmatched coverage across its expanding retail footprint. In 1996, it launched its Commercial Programme, directly serving repair shops and creating a high-frequency, B2B revenue stream.

Exclusive supplier partnerships secured access to in-demand products competitors couldn't easily replicate, while logistics efficiency reinforced AutoZone's reputation as a dependable partner. These base camp years established the infrastructure, supplier network and customer relationships that would sustain AutoZone's compounding trajectory for decades.

Royal Enfield (2005–2010): Igniting the Bullet Rebellion

The years between 2005 and 2010 marked Royal Enfield's base camp, the decisive period when Siddhartha Lal transformed a fading legacy into a cultural movement. After becoming CEO in 2000, Lal divested 13 underperforming businesses by 2005, freeing capital and focus for Royal Enfield's revival. With sharper retro styling, modernised manufacturing and reliable platforms, the brand retained its heritage while gaining newfound credibility.

Equally important was the creation of community. Riding clubs, flagship events like Rider Mania, and leisure-riding campaigns reframed Royal Enfield as more than a motorcycle – it was an identity. By 2010, sales had grown nearly sixfold, from ~50,000 units in 2005 to close to 300,000. The combination of operational focus, cultural revival, and emotional branding built the foundation for Royal Enfield's compounding journey – a base camp that set the climb towards becoming a 100x story.

Field Guide: Scaling Physical Moats

Company	Base Camp Phase	TAM	Moat
Home Depot	1985–1990: Store rollout and supply chain edge	US Home Improvement	Scale + Service + Cost Leadership
Walmart	1975–1986: Regional to national logistics powerhouse	Mass Retail	Cost Efficiency + Vendor Scale
AutoZone	1995–2001: Supply chain reinvestment	Auto Parts Retail	Supply Chain + Store Density
Eicher Motors: Royal Enfield	2005–2010: Mid-sized motorcycle revival	Premium Motorcycles	Brand Power + Cultural Identity

Owning the Network Effects

Booking Holdings (2000–2007): From Opaque Bids to Global Travel Powerhouse

Between 2000 and 2007, Priceline transformed from a niche bidding site into a scalable global travel marketplace. It shifted beyond opaque auctions into merchant and retail hotel listings, built direct property relationships, and invested heavily in SEO, becoming synonymous with online travel discovery.

Two acquisitions defined this base camp phase: Active Hotels (2004), which brought tens of thousands of European properties, and Booking.com (2005), whose intuitive platform and SEO dominance meshed seamlessly with Priceline's marketing machine. Together, they created a flywheel of supply, reviews and direct bookings that no rival could match.

By the rebound after the dot-com crash and 9/11, Priceline had reinvented itself as Booking Holdings, a diversified international platform with the infrastructure, brand and geographic reach to fuel decades of compounding. This was its *base camp*: the gritty formative years where reinvestment and strategic acquisitions set the stage for a 100× climb.

Field Guide – Owning the Network Effects

Company	Base Camp Phase	TAM	Moat
Booking Holdings	2000–2007: Global travel aggregation buildout	Global Travel & Experiences	Network Effects + Platform Scale

How Long Does the Base Camp Period Last?

Recognising Base Camp is only half the battle. The real challenge? Having the patience to endure it.

Typically, the Base Camp phase lasts four to eight years. During this period:

- The company has achieved early traction but not broad dominance.
- It is aggressively reinvesting in logistics, brand, moats, and infrastructure.
- Margins are compressed, and cash flows are often reinvested at unattractive rates.
- Scepticism and volatility remain high, with the market doubting scalability and durability.
- Valuations appear expensive relative to today's numbers, but cheap relative to future potential.
- Strategic acquisitions and alliances are common; companies like Booking Holdings, Microsoft, FICO, Ansys, AutoZone and Monster have used this phase to buy capabilities, expand their TAM, strengthen moats and reshape their business models for the long run.

Key Insight:

Base Camp feels slow when you're living through it, but in hindsight, it's where the foundation for the 100x journey is quietly laid.

Typical Phases Within Base Camp

Stage	Characteristics
Early (Years 1–3)	Finding repeatable product-market fit; heavy reinvestment; low margins; high volatility; small bolt-on acquisitions to fill product gaps or strengthen supply chain.
Middle (Years 3–5)	TAM expansion becomes visible; brand strength and economies of scale emerge; acquisitions target adjacent markets, new geographies, or complementary tech; alliances deepen customer and partner lock-in.

Stage	Characteristics
Late (Years 5–8)	Early signs of operating leverage; margin expansion begins; analyst coverage improves but conviction is still required; acquisitions now focus on scaling distribution or accelerating monetization.

Base Camp Is a Mental Game

Most investors bail out during Base Camp, often right before the climb steepens. Patience through this phase separates the 5× winners from the 100× legends.

Analogy:

Base Camp is like building the foundation of a skyscraper. It feels invisible and slow, but once ready, the tower rises faster than anyone expects.

Key Lessons from Base Camp

Across industries, winners display recurring patterns during this phase:

- Reinvestment precedes margins – companies pour cash into capabilities long before Wall Street rewards them.
- TAM expansion often starts quietly – into new geographies, adjacent categories, or platform layers.
- Moats are built operationally – via distribution, data, brand equity, or embedded standards – and rarely announced in press releases.
- Acquisitions and alliances seed long-term dominance – early M&A and partnerships lock in customers, extend reach, and integrate the company deeper into its ecosystem.
- Valuation optics mislead – what looks expensive on current metrics is often cheap on forward unit economics.

- Time is the edge – the hardest but most valuable skill is holding through volatility when the crowd mistakes it for fragility.

Investor Takeaways: Why Base Camp Matters

For investors, Base Camp is the rarest and most rewarding time to enter a position. Growth potential is high, competition hasn't fully mobilised, and the company is quietly building capabilities the market undervalues. Spotting these moments means looking past quarterly earnings and focusing on the quality of moats, reinvestment runways, and management's willingness to delay gratification.

The greatest fortunes are made by investing at Base Camp and staying the course until the company reaches the summit.

CHAPTER

10

The TAM vs Moat Matrix: How to Combine Scale with Defensibility

"Scale economics shared incentivises customer reciprocation, and customer reciprocation is a super-factor in business performance."
— ***Nick Sleep, Nomad Investment Partnership Letters.***

Imagine two mountaineers preparing for very different climbs.

- The first has top-tier gear including ice axes, crampons and satellite navigation, but is standing in front of a tiny 500-foot hill.
- The second faces Everest but is ill-equipped.

Neither will achieve anything remarkable, the first because the challenge is too small, the second because the challenge is overwhelming.

Now picture a climber with the same elite equipment standing at the foot of Everest. That perfect pairing of world-class capability and world-class opportunity is where 100-bagger returns are born.

This metaphor captures the essence of the TAM vs Moat Matrix, a two-by-two mental model designed to sharpen an investor's judgement. It forces us to examine not just the size of the opportunity (TAM) but also the company's ability to defend and expand within it (moat). In Terminal Value Investing, the holy grail is to find businesses operating in vast, expanding markets with competitive moats that grow stronger over time.

The Four Quadrants of the TAM vs Moat Matrix

Quadrant	Description	Example Companies
TAM Trapped	Small TAM, Weak Moat, low ceiling, little protection	Dish TV, Blockbuster
Niche Fortress	Small TAM, Strong Moat, stable but limited upside	Moody's, See's Candies, CME Group
Hype Mirage	Large TAM, Weak Moat, tempting story, poor durability	WeWork, Yahoo, BlackBerry
The Everest Zone	Large TAM, Strong Moat, rare compounding machines	Amazon, Apple, Netflix, Titan

TAM Trapped: Small Market, Weak Moat

This is the danger zone for investors chasing early excitement without considering long-term scalability. These businesses often operate in mature or structurally limited markets and lack defensible moats.

Blockbuster is a cautionary tale. Once dominant in video rentals, it relied on a physical footprint as its 'moat' but ignored the shift in consumer behaviour and the expanding TAM of digital streaming. Netflix didn't just compete; it redefined the category.

Dish TV, similarly, led India's DTH wave, but its addressable market was constrained by low ARPU and growing competition from internet-based streaming. Without pricing power or proprietary content, Dish couldn't build lasting loyalty or scale with industry shifts.

These companies may have had early momentum, but lacked the two ingredients essential for long-term compounding: a scalable market and a defensible edge.

Niche Fortress: Small Market, Strong Moat

These businesses are the equivalent of medieval castles — high walls and narrow gates, sitting atop limited terrain. You won't get 100x returns here, but you may get consistent compounding and a defensive portfolio anchor.

Moody's is the textbook example. The TAM for credit ratings is relatively small, but Moody's moat — regulatory endorsement, legacy databases, and deep integration into fixed income markets — is near-impossible to replicate.

See's Candies built an enduring fortress by pairing meticulous, small-batch quality with nostalgic brand storytelling and a tightly controlled West Coast retail footprint. The overall TAM for boxed chocolates is modest, but See's converts fanatical customer loyalty and premium pricing into decades of high-margin cash flow, proving a narrow moat can still be extraordinarily durable.

Hype Mirage: Large Market, Weak Moat

This is the quadrant that lures countless investors. The market is vast, the narrative is seductive, and early growth metrics look exciting. But beneath the surface, the business lacks a durable competitive edge. Without a moat, its position cannot be sustained; what begins as promise often unravels into disappointment.

BlackBerry once had the mobile enterprise world at its feet. Its secure email and QWERTY keyboard were iconic. But as Apple and Android introduced better platforms and ecosystems, BlackBerry's lack of adaptability became fatal. Its moat, once rooted in hardware, was quickly rendered obsolete by software and UX innovation.

Yahoo, similarly, had traffic, content and brand value but no product coherence, no sustainable lock-in and slow execution. Google out-searched it. Facebook out-networked it. The TAM was massive but the moat was leaky.

The Everest Zone: Large Market, Strong Moat

This is the summit. The rare quadrant where truly legendary investments are born. These companies don't just operate in massive TAMs — they expand them. And they do so while deepening their moats through scale, data, brand equity, or reinvestment loops.

Amazon started in books, a niche, but reinvested relentlessly in global commerce, fulfilment, AWS, and Prime. Its TAM went from retail to global logistics and cloud infrastructure. Its moat? Unmatched infrastructure, flywheels, and switching costs.

Apple disrupted phones, created an app economy, expanded into wearables, and now commands a multi-trillion-dollar ecosystem. Its vertical integration, brand power, and ecosystem stickiness are among the strongest moats in the world.

Netflix began mailing DVDs. It transitioned to streaming, then to content creation, and now competes for global attention. Its moat is a unique combination of content, data and user habit.

Titan formalised a fragmented jewellery market in India. Its brand became synonymous with trust. It reinvested in design, customer experience and operational discipline, turning cultural behaviour into a durable moat.

Why the Matrix Matters

The Matrix helps investors resist the allure of short-term growth stories and redirect focus towards long-term compounding potential. It asks two essential questions:

- Is the market large enough to support decades of growth?
- Does the company have a defensible edge that will strengthen over time?

If the answer to both is yes, you may be looking at your next Everest.

Investor Takeaways – The Summit Filter

Before hitting 'Buy', plot the business on this matrix. Ask yourself: Is this a TAM Trapped story dressed as growth? A niche fortress that'll stagnate? A hype train missing moats? Or is this a true climber scaling Everest with an ice axe in hand?

Because the world's best returns aren't earned in any market – they're earned in the Everest Zone.

PART II

ENGINES OF COMPOUNDING

CHAPTER

11 Optionality and Second Base Camp

"Optionality is the property of asymmetric upside (preferably unlimited) with correspondingly limited downside (preferably tiny)."
— ***Nassim Nicholas Taleb, Antifragile***

Some companies scale a mountain. The truly exceptional ones find another peak behind it and climb again. This chapter explores how great companies reinvent themselves by exercising optionality: the strategic pursuit of new opportunities that extend growth beyond the core. These are second base camps – new inflection points that prolong the climb.

ONE MOUNTAIN CLIMBED. ANOTHER DISCOVERED

What Is Optionality in Business?

Optionality refers to a company's ability to pivot, expand or create new revenue streams, often using the strength of its existing base. It's the opposite of stagnation. Optionality compounds growth through reinvention, adjacency and ecosystem thinking.

Optionality can be:

- Product-led (Apple's iPod to iPhone)
- Market-led (Netflix moving from US DVD to global streaming)
- Strategic M&A (Coca-Cola acquiring Minute Maid, Costa Coffee, Fairlife to expand its non-soda TAM)
- Platform-led (Amazon expanded from e-commerce to cloud, content and logistics through AWS, Prime and acquisitions)
- Cloud and AI-led (Microsoft transformed from a Windows-first company to a cloud and enterprise AI powerhouse through Azure, Office 365, Copilot and OpenAI integration)
- AI and Ecosystem-led (Nvidia evolved from a GPU maker for gaming to the backbone of AI, powering data centres, autonomous vehicles, robotics, and enterprise AI platforms through CUDA, DGX, and partnerships)
- Brand-led (Titan scaled from watches to jewellery, eyewear and ethnic wear, while expanding through sub-brands like Mia and CaratLane, and launching Taneira in apparel)

Let's explore how some of the world's greatest businesses created new base camps after their initial climbs.

Apple: From Device Maker to Ecosystem Engine

Apple's iPhone didn't just succeed; it unlocked entirely new growth vectors. The App Store (2008) created a platform economy that scaled into services (subscriptions, iCloud, Music), fintech (Apple Pay, Wallet) and hardware adjacencies (Apple Watch, AirPods). Each vertical represented a new 'summit', layered atop the iPhone base.

This optionality was powered by reinvestment and integration. Services now generate recurring revenue streams, wearables have become billion-dollar businesses, and Apple is expanding into health and payments. What began with the iPod evolved into an ecosystem worth over $3 trillion by 2025, proof that optionality, when built on a strong base camp, can compound into a digital empire.

Microsoft: From Office Suite to Cloud Behemoth

Microsoft's first act was defined by Windows and Office. By the early 2010s, growth had plateaued. Under Satya Nadella, the company repositioned itself around Azure, its cloud computing platform. It shifted from licence sales to SaaS, from desktop to enterprise, from margin defence to bold reinvestment.

Azure became a second base camp, with server products and cloud services growing to over $97 billion in annualised revenue. Microsoft also extended optionality into:

- LinkedIn (acquisition)
- GitHub (developer ecosystem)
- Microsoft Teams (collaboration)
- OpenAI partnership (AI integration across Office and Azure)

From 2014 to 2025, Microsoft's market cap grew 10x.

Netflix: From Distribution to Content to Gaming

Netflix's story is one of successive reinventions. Its first act was DVD distribution. Its second was streaming, which enabled global expansion. Its third was becoming a content producer, creating original IP that fuelled both subscriber loyalty and licensing revenue. By the 2020s, Netflix pursued its fourth act: gaming.

Acquisitions like Night School Studio and Next Games marked its push into interactive entertainment, aiming to extend engagement beyond passive viewing. Its subscriber base grew from 20M in 2010 to over 300M by 2024. Netflix could leverage its distribution, brand, and personalisation engine to scale gaming as another optionality layer. Each reinvention — distribution → streaming → content → gaming—added fresh avenues for growth, keeping the company ahead of Disney+, Prime Video, and newer challengers.

Coca-Cola: From Soda Giant to Beverage Empire

Coca-Cola's original moat was built on a century of brand, distribution and pricing power. But as soda consumption slowed, the company reinvented its growth avenues through acquisitions, product diversification and strategic tie-ups:

- Costa Coffee: a $5.1 billion acquisition in 2019, giving Coca-Cola a strong global platform in hot beverages.
- Bodyarmor: full acquisition in 2021, expanding into premium sports drinks to compete with Gatorade.
- Coca-Cola Zero and Diet Coke: catering to health-conscious consumers and extending the life of the flagship brand.
- Smartwater, Dasani, and sparkling waters: capturing the fast-growing bottled water and flavoured sparkling segments.
- Minute Maid, Simply, and local juices: tapping into fruit-based beverages and regionally tailored tastes.
- Fairlife (Milk & Dairy): a majority stake in 2020, entering value-added dairy and protein-rich drinks.

- Monster Beverage tie-up: a strategic partnership and 16% equity stake in 2015, giving Coca-Cola exposure to the global energy drinks market without directly competing with Monster's edgy brand identity.

Through this mosaic of categories including coffee, sports drinks, water, juice, dairy and energy, Coca-Cola has extended its TAM and moat beyond carbonated soft drinks, leveraging its unparalleled distribution system to stay relevant in changing consumer landscapes.

Amazon: Optionality at Scale

From its start as an online bookstore, Amazon leveraged its platform and infrastructure to enter and often redefine entire industries. AWS emerged as the most powerful example of turning internal capabilities outward, creating the world's most profitable cloud business.

Optionality extended further: Prime Video in streaming, Kindle and Echo in devices, Whole Foods in physical retail, its own delivery chain in logistics, and now AI tools such as Bedrock and Amazon LLMs. Each new venture drew on Amazon's core strengths: platform thinking, customer obsession, and a fulfilment network that doubled as a launchpad for category after category. This second base camp gave Amazon the structural ability to keep creating growth engines far beyond its original domain.

Nvidia: From Gaming Chips to the Backbone of AI

Nvidia's most powerful trait has been optionality. Starting as a gaming GPU company, it transformed into the infrastructure layer of the AI economy. CUDA turned GPUs into programmable compute engines, enabling Nvidia to enter adjacencies ranging from

AI training to robotics, autonomous driving, cloud supercomputing and industrial simulation.

Optionality flourished through ecosystem thinking. Products like DGX AI supercomputers, enterprise AI platforms, and Omniverse for digital twins show how Nvidia leveraged its platform into entirely new verticals. Partnerships with hyperscalers, OpenAI, Microsoft, Tesla, and AWS embedded its chips at the centre of generative AI, healthcare imaging, and autonomous systems.

This second base camp illustrates Nvidia's ability to continuously reinvent itself: from gaming champion to AI kingmaker to a trillion-dollar ecosystem enabler, with multiple growth runways still ahead.

Titan: Building New Verticals on a Strong Base

With jewellery as its anchor, Titan has pursued disciplined optionality. It launched Mia for affordable modern designs, acquired CaratLane to build digital and omnichannel strength, and expanded Tanishq into Dubai, Abu Dhabi, and the US, early steps towards a global Indian jewellery brand. Beyond jewellery, Titan extended into eyewear (Titan Eye+), fragrances (Skinn), and ethnic wear (Taneira), leveraging its brand trust, retail know-how, and design DNA. Each move represents a 'second base camp': an adjacent category scaled with discipline, turning optionality into durable, high-margin growth engines.

Patterns of Optionality

Across all these stories, we find common traits:

- Core cash flow reinvested into adjacent bets
- Second base camps unlock new TAMs

- Bold pivots before the core is exhausted
- Willingness to cannibalize own products

Optionality requires not just capital but vision. It's about climbing a new mountain even while dominating the old one.

Investor Takeaways - The Second Summit

Optionality isn't always obvious. But the signs include:

- Large, profitable core
- New product or M&A experimentation
- Customer adjacencies being tested
- Early traction in new verticals

These second summits are what allow great companies to outlast cycles and remain relevant for decades.

As a Terminal Value Investor, identifying companies that have the will and ability to reinvent themselves is the ultimate edge.

CHAPTER

12

Changing Customer Behaviour – The Hidden Engine of TAM Expansion

I think there will be 20 years of evolution from linear broadcast to internet television.

— ***Reed Hastings***

Most investors treat Total Addressable Market (TAM) as a number, fixed, measurable and immutable. But the world's most valuable companies didn't just find large markets – they made them bigger by fundamentally changing how people think, act and consume.

Behaviour change is the hidden engine of TAM expansion. It is what turns a niche offering into a mass habit. These companies didn't wait for demand – they created it.

CONSUMER BEHAVIOUR CHANGING OVER THE YEARS

MARKETS DON'T JUST GROW - PEOPLE CHANGE, AND MARKETS FOLLOW.

Infosys: Turning IT from Cost Centre to Strategic Asset

In the 1990s and early 2000s, companies saw IT as a support function – costly, internal, and often inefficient. Infosys helped global businesses rethink IT as a scalable, strategic partner, pioneering offshore development, 24/7 support, and enterprise-wide transformation.

Behaviour Shift: From in-house IT to globalised, managed services.

Result: TAM expanded from software maintenance to digital transformation, consulting, ERP implementation, and AI integration, creating an entire $250B+ Indian IT services sector.

Apple: Turning Tech into Identity

Before 2007, phones were just communication tools. Then Apple introduced the iPhone, a breakthrough that fused touchscreen design, hardware-software integration, and intuitive UX into a single object of desire.

The iPhone wasn't just a product; it was a personal portal to connection, content, creativity, commerce and more. Apple didn't just build devices. It made technology emotional, personal and aspirational.

Behaviour Shift:

From using phones as functional tools → to living through them as lifestyle companions.
The phone became:

- A camera
- A wallet

- A social hub
- A health tracker
- A content studio
- And eventually – a digital identity extension

TAM Expansion:

What started as a computer company turned into a consumer tech giant by:

- Moving from computers to phones to wearables, subscriptions, payments, smart homes, and health tech.
- Creating an ecosystem so sticky that hardware sales drove services growth, and vice versa.
- Building an emotional brand that delivered premium pricing power, recurring revenues and low churn.

Apple didn't just capture demand — it shaped it.
It showed how product design and behavioural insight can expand TAM far beyond the original market.

Amazon: Rewriting Retail Norms

Amazon's genius wasn't just in selling books. It built trust in an untrusted space – e-commerce – and then made that trust habitual. With one-click orders, fast shipping, and customer obsession, Amazon turned 'online shopping' into the default shopping method.

Behaviour Shift: From store-first to screen-first.

Result: TAM exploded across every consumer vertical – retail, logistics, cloud (AWS), and content (Prime Video).

Netflix - Bingeing as Behaviour

Netflix saw that entertainment didn't need to be scheduled. By enabling streaming, recommending content, and dropping entire seasons at once, it gave users control over their time and habits, creating a cultural shift.

Behaviour Shift: From watching on schedule to watching on demand.

Result: TAM expanded from DVDs to a global, multi-billion-dollar streaming economy.

Titan (Tanishq) - Professionalizing Jewellery

Gold buying in India was informal, based on family-run stores and bargaining. Titan's Tanishq brought trust, elegance and professionalism to jewellery. With purity certifications and organised retail, it made buying gold feel like buying brands.

Behaviour Shift: From tradition-bound to fashion-conscious, especially among women and youth.

Result: TAM expanded from ceremonial gold to everyday fashion, opening up massive organised jewellery and lifestyle markets.

Walmart: Democratizing Everyday Affordability

In the 1980s, retail was either premium or fragmented. Walmart pioneered 'Everyday Low Prices', offering predictable affordability. It brought modern retail to underserved towns, reconditioning rural America to prioritise bulk savings and one-stop access.

Behaviour Shift: From brand loyalty to value loyalty. From shopping around to shopping once.

Result: TAM grew from general goods to groceries, pharmacy and e-commerce. Walmart became the backbone of household consumption.

Home Depot - Creating the DIY Culture

Home improvement was once the contractor's domain. Home Depot gave consumers the tools, guidance and confidence to build themselves. With how-to content, knowledgeable staff and massive product variety, it empowered millions of non-pros.

Behaviour Shift: From hire-it-out to do-it-yourself.

Result: TAM expanded beyond trade professionals to hobbyists, homeowners, and tech-savvy renovators.

Booking Holdings: Normalizing Online Travel

Booking a hotel room once meant phone calls, travel agents, or waiting at check-in counters. Booking Holdings changed that by making online travel booking intuitive, instant and trustworthy. With real-time inventory, guest reviews, price comparisons and easy cancellation, it shifted travel planning from a chore to a click. Travellers began trusting algorithms over agents.

Behaviour Shift: From offline and agent-led to self-serve digital booking.

Result: TAM expanded from business and affluent travellers to millions of digital-first users across income tiers, geographies, and trip types, hotels, rentals, and beyond.

Eicher Motors: Royal Enfield: Romanticising the Ride

Mid-sized motorcycles were once viewed as impractical and niche, caught between commuter bikes and premium imports. Royal Enfield redefined this category by turning motorcycling into an aspirational lifestyle. With retro-styled bikes, thumping engines and a focus on the ride experience, it elevated biking from utility to identity. The brand invested in riding clubs, merchandise and experiential retail that connected emotionally with young urban consumers.

Behaviour Shift: From two wheeler as a transport to motorcycling-as-self-expression.
Result: Sales expanded from ₹255 crore in 2008 to over ₹16536 crore by 2025 driven by lifestyle adoption across India and emerging export markets.

Bajaj Finance: Making Credit Aspirational

Credit in India was once complex, slow, and available only to a privileged few. Bajaj Finance changed that by offering fast, accessible financing, especially for first-time borrowers buying consumer durables. Through EMI cards, point-of-sale financing, and zero-cost EMIs, it made borrowing feel less like debt and more like empowerment. The firm demystified credit for the masses and brought millions into the formal lending system.

Behaviour Shift: From credit-averse and paperwork-heavy to instant, embedded financing.

Result: TAM exploded from a ₹1.85 lakh crore retail credit market in 2008 to ₹22 lakh crore by 2025, as more consumers became credit-active and digitally enabled.

Investor Takeaway – Behaviour Is the Real TAM Multiplier

Most investors treat TAM as a fixed number. But the best companies prove it's fluid, stretchable by shaping how people behave.

These companies didn't just forecast growth; they created it by:

- Reframing what customers value and trust
- Normalizing new habits and routines
- Solving ignored pain points
- Building emotional resonance that drives loyalty

Key Insight:

Behaviour change compounds.
It shifts consumption from occasional to habitual, from functional to emotional. That transition isn't just sticky, it's exponential. It leads to:

- New category creation
- Recurring revenues
- Durable pricing power
- Moats based on habit, not hype

What Smart Investors Ask:

"What could the TAM become if this new behaviour goes mainstream?"

Because TAM isn't a boundary, it's a by-product of human change.

From Habits to Terminal Value

Owning behaviour is owning the future. When a company becomes part of a customer's routine, it doesn't just earn revenue — it earns resilience.

So when you model Terminal Value, don't just extrapolate current trends.

Ask: What new norms are being formed today that will shape tomorrow's cash flows?

That's where compounding truly lives.

Investor Takeaways

TAM isn't fixed; it's flexible. And customer behaviour is what bends it.

Most investors see Total Addressable Market as a cap. But in reality, the best companies don't just meet demand; they create it by transforming how people think, act and buy.

Behaviour isn't just a growth lever – it's the real TAM expander.

CHAPTER 13

Margins - The Secret Engine Behind Terminal Value

"Profit is not the purpose of a business,
but rather the test of its validity."

— Peter F. Drucker.

In the Everest of Investing, sheer revenue growth alone does not carry a business to the summit. True and lasting wealth creation happens when a company scales its top line and steadily strengthens its foundation through Operating Profit Margin (OPM) expansion.

Margins are the hidden engines of Terminal Value. While top-line growth captures attention, it is margin expansion that quietly transforms a promising company into a relentless compounding machine. A rising OPM amplifies a business's ability to self-fund innovation, deepen moats, build resilience, undertake reinvestment and navigate shocks — all without depending on external capital.

Even modest margin improvements can sharply bend the compounding curve upwards, turning linear growth into exponential wealth creation.

"A small shift in margins can create a massive shift in wealth."

Margin expansion isn't accidental. It signals strategic clarity, operational discipline, pricing power, and the advantage of scale economies. It is the mark of a company maturing from adolescent promise to fortress-like dominance.

In this chapter, we examine how some of the greatest long-term compounders – Amazon, Apple, Moutai, ASML, Ansys, FICO, Monster Beverage, Netflix, AutoZone, Eicher Motors, Booking Holdings and Bajaj Finance – began at Base Camp with modest margins, yet steadily maintained or expanded profitability as they scaled.

Margin improvement is not merely a financial outcome; it reflects strategic maturity. When margin expansion converges with expanding TAM (Total Addressable Market) and intelligent reinvestment, it becomes the ultimate catalyst for 50x, 100x, even 500x returns.

In the Everest of Investing, it's not enough to grow taller; you must grow stronger. And nothing signals hidden strength like expanding margins.

The Quiet Power of Margin Expansion

The table below showcases how some of the world's greatest compounders didn't just grow their top line; they structurally improved their profitability over time. Many started with razor-thin or even negative margins. But through scale, efficiency, pricing power, product mix evolution and operating leverage, they transformed their economics dramatically. These margin transformations didn't happen overnight, but over decades they became the hidden flywheel behind shareholder returns.

Table 5: Operating Margin Expansion

Company (Base → Current Year)	Base OPM	Current OPM	Δ (pts)	Key Driver
Microsoft (Jun-86 → Jun-25)	19%	45%	+26	Mix tilted from boxed software to Azure and SaaS suites
Titan (Mar-01 → Mar-25)	10%	9%	-1	Jewellery mix compressed margins
Amazon (Dec-97 → Dec-24)	-19%	10%	+29	AWS, Prime, logistics leverage
HDFC Bank (PBT) (Mar-98 → Mar-25)	33%	20%	-13	Retail mix & tech spend
Apple (Sep-01 → Sep-24)	-6%	32%	+38	iPhone + Services mix
Kweichow Moutai (Dec-02 → Dec-24)	35%	67%	+32	Premium pricing & scarcity
Infosys (Mar-98 → Mar-25)	25%	21%	-4	Wage & pricing pressure
ASML (Dec-95 → Dec-24)	23%	32%	+9	EUV monopoly economics
NVIDIA (Jan-16 → Jan-25)	15%	61%	+46	AI GPU pricing power
AutoZone (Aug-95 → Aug-24)	12%	20%	+8	Private-label + logistics
Netflix (Dec-02 → Dec-24)	-7%	27%	+34	Streaming scale & originals
Monster Beverage (Dec-02 → Dec-24)	6%	26%	+20	Brand & co-packing model
Home Depot (Jan-85 → Feb-25)	6%	5%	-1	Wage and omni-channel capex
Walmart (Jan-75 → Jan-25)	5%	4%	-1	EDLP & e-commerce drag
Ansys (Dec-00 → Dec-24)	26%	28%	+2	Subscription licences
FICO (Sep-00 → Sep-24)	15%	43%	+31	Decision-analytics SaaS

Company (Base → Current Year)	Base OPM	Current OPM	Δ (pts)	Key Driver
Eicher Motors (Mar-08 → Mar-25)	-8%	21%	+29	Royal Enfield premiumisation
Booking Holdings (Dec-00 → Dec-24)	-26%	32%	+58	Asset-light OTA model
Bajaj Finance (PBT) (Mar-10 → Mar-25)	15%	32%	+17	Tech-led underwriting & fees

What the Outliers Teach

- Positive swingers: Booking Holdings, NVIDIA, Apple, show how platform economics or category dominance can add 30–50 margin points with surprisingly little incremental capital.
- Flat/negative movers – Titan, Walmart – remind us that category mix, wage pressure, or strategic reinvestment can cap margins even in stellar businesses; great compounders can still come from revenue scale and capital efficiency.
- Rule of thumb: a sustained 10-point margin lift on steady revenue can double operating profit, often the hidden engine behind the market's "compounders" club.

A few giants — Titan, HDFC Bank, Home Depot, Walmart, Infosys — show flat or slightly lower margins, proving that expansion is not guaranteed; it must be earned through strategic mix shifts, pricing power and relentless cost discipline.

Take-aways

1. Mix matters: Shifting towards subscription, platform or ultra-premium products (AWS, App Store) widens gross margins and drops straight to the bottom line.
2. Scale breeds efficiency: asset turns, fixed-cost absorption and network effects (Booking, Netflix, Amazon logistics) magnify incremental profits.

3. Capital discipline wins: Companies like Bajaj Finance and Monster proved that lean distribution and technology leverage can expand margins even in seemingly mature categories.
4. Operating leverage compounds value: a 5-point margin lift on steady revenue doubles profit; the 20- to 50-point jumps above are why these businesses became legendary compounders.

Revenue growth excites, but sustained margin expansion is the stealth engine that turns good businesses into unstoppable wealth-creating machines.

Target OPM: the Margin That Turns Growth into Fortunes

When you size up a young, high-growth firm, don't lock onto today's slim margins. Ask what operating-profit margin (OPM) the company can earn once it is large, steady, and past its heavy spend phase. That "Target OPM" appears after:

1. Reinvestment slows to a normal rhythm,
2. Fixed costs are spread across a much bigger base, and
3. Pricing power and brand strength kick in.

Project that end state margin and not the current one because it drives almost all of the terminal value in a discounted cash flow model.

Why Target OPM Matters

Revenue growth supplies the fuel, whereas Target OPM is the engine that converts fuel to speed. A higher eventual margin:

- throws off more cash to fund the next growth wave,
- cushions the business in downturns, and
- Let's free cash flow compound at turbo-speed.

How to Analyse Target OPM Practically

Benchmark Against Industry Leaders:

Study mature companies in the same sector to set realistic margin expectations. For example, Amazon's early investors benchmarked against Walmart's 4% to 5% retail margins, while today's digital ad platforms like Meta and Alphabet sustain 35% to 40% OPM. Luxury brands like LVMH consistently operate at 25% to 30% margins, proof of the pricing power premium brands can command.

Adjust for Scale Effects:

Recognise that early-stage businesses often suffer low margins due to heavy investments in logistics, R&D, and customer acquisition. As they scale, these fixed costs flatten out, and operating leverage naturally improves.

Watch for Signs of Emerging Pricing Power:

Early indicators like rising Average Revenue Per User (ARPU), successful premiumisation, or falling customer churn signal that margin expansion may be ahead.

Evaluate Reinvestment Behaviour:

Healthy businesses willingly sacrifice short-term margins to build long-term competitive moats, whether through ecosystem investments, infrastructure build-out, or product innovation. Reluctance to invest often signals a weak growth runway.

Stay Patient:

Margin expansion is rarely linear. It often unfolds quietly over five to ten years as reinvestments mature and operating leverage kicks in. Quarter-to-quarter results may stay noisy, but underneath, the compounding machinery is building.

Investor Takeaways - The Margin Is the Multiplier

Growth is exciting, but profitability at scale is what turns growth into generational wealth. Model the target OPM and you'll understand why the biggest winners look deceptively expensive, right before their margins break out and the real compounding begins.

CHAPTER

14

From Unit Economics to Terminal Value

Unit economics form the underpinning of any venture's financial model."
— ***Bret Waters, writing on Medium***

Valuation is about connecting the dots between a company's economic model and the ability to generate future cash flows. When each transaction funds the climb.

When Jeff Bezos started Amazon as an online bookstore in 1995, the business barely made money on each book sold. It was a high-volume, low-margin play. But hidden inside each transaction was something much more powerful than a few cents of profit: the blueprint for a compounding engine. Welcome to the critical but often overlooked bridge between micro and macro – Unit Economics to Terminal Value.

Most investors focus on high-level financials: revenue growth, EBITDA margins and free cash flow. But the seeds of terminal value are planted in the trenches at the unit level. How much does it cost to acquire a customer (CAC)? What is their lifetime value (LTV)? What are the contribution margins? And perhaps most importantly: is each transaction building a foundation for compounding, or simply burning capital?

Amazon: The Poster Child of Unit-Level Compounding

In the late 1990s, Amazon was losing money on paper. But a closer look at unit economics revealed its genius. With every book sold, Amazon:

- Acquired a customer cheaply via word of mouth or SEO.
- Delivered fast, frictionless service.
- Earned repeat purchases, increasing customer LTV.

Bezos didn't just want to sell books; he wanted to build trust and habit. The long-term game was clear: repeat purchases would reduce CAC (customer acquisition cost), boost LTV to CAC ratios, and create massive operating leverage. The flywheel began to turn.

That unit-level discipline enabled Amazon to reinvest:

- Into logistics infrastructure (Fulfilment by Amazon)
- Into customer loyalty (Amazon Prime)
- Into new TAMs (AWS, Kindle, Alexa)

By 2024, Amazon wasn't just a retailer. It was an infrastructure layer for global commerce and cloud computing, with AWS alone delivering ~37% operating profit margins and funding further innovation.

From Micro Margins to Macro Moats

The path from good unit economics to terminal value typically follows four stages:

1. Contribution Margin Positive:
    - Each unit sold covers variable costs and contributes to fixed cost recovery.

- Example: Zomato's food delivery segment reached over 4.4% OPM in Q4 FY25 by optimising delivery costs and restaurant partnerships.

2. LTV > CAC with Retention:
   - Customers keep coming back. Reacquisition costs fall.
   - Netflix built stickiness through content personalisation and binge behaviour.
3. Operating Leverage Kicks In

Revenue scales faster than fixed costs.

Tesla leveraged its massive upfront investment in Giga factories, R&D, and software to improve margins as vehicle deliveries scaled. Once production ramped up, fixed costs such as factory operations and software development were spread over a growing volume base, leading to strong margin expansion.

Reinvestment into New TAMs:

- Profits are funnelled into new verticals, categories, or geographies.
- Amazon turned retail profits into AWS. Apple used iPod cash flows to fund the iPhone, App Store, etc.

Investor Lens: What to Watch For

When evaluating an early-stage or scaling business, ask:

- Is the contribution margin positive and expanding?
- How long does it take to break even per user or transaction?
- Is the company reinvesting profits into structural moats or just spending on acquisition?
- Are unit-level margins funding long-term terminal value?

A company with great unit economics but poor capital allocation may never reach the summit. Conversely, a company with thin early margins but strong reinvestment discipline may become a compounding machine.

Case Snapshots

- Netflix: From DVD rentals to streaming and original content. Every subscriber added was a margin-expanding asset, especially as content scaled across geographies.
- Apple: Every iPod sold funded iPhone R&D. Every iPhone sale added users to an ecosystem now monetised via services at over 70% gross margin.
- Eternal (India): Zomato's core food-delivery business is set to clear the 5% Operating Margin to Gross Order Value mark soon. Management is recycling that cash into higher-velocity, higher-margin bets, Quick Commerce (Blinkit) and the 'Going Out' discovery layer (District). The company's innovation lab keeps pushing out tools like Nugget whilst fine-tuning restaurant ops and retention loops. Food delivery already prints profits; the open question for investors is whether these adjacent wagers will compound rather than dilute that success.

Investor Takeaways – The Maths Behind the Magic

Unit economics aren't just for founders and operators. They are vital for long-term investors, because every 100x stock began as a single transaction with a positive margin, strong retention, and the discipline to reinvest wisely.

Terminal Value is not magic. It is maths, multiplied by time, and funded one transaction at a time.

CHAPTER 15

The Blind Spot: Why Most Models Never Catch the 100x Climb

"The greatest shortcoming of the human race is our inability to understand the exponential function."

—Albert A. Bartlett

It isn't that investors miss the numbers; they miss the story those numbers are quietly telling. In investing, the most dangerous blind spot isn't ignorance, it's incompleteness. Most investors miss 100x returns not because they can't identify great businesses. They miss them because their models are too short-term and their patience too short-lived. Some fail to see the full arc of greatness. Others see it, but walk away too soon.

This chapter explores both these traps: why most models fail to capture the real shape of a compounding journey, and why most investors exit before the magic fully unfolds.

The Forecast Fallacy: Why Most Models Miss the Real Climb

One of the most persistent blind spots in investing is the Forecast Fallacy: the belief that a business's future can be neatly captured within a five- to ten-year model. Most discounted cash flow analyses and sell-side projections are built around this narrow horizon, followed by a static terminal growth rate. The result is structurally conservative but critically flawed when applied to the world's most transformative companies. True compounders rarely follow predictable arcs. They expand TAMs, unlock second and third growth curves, and create optionality that no model can foresee in advance. Amazon's leap from books to cloud computing, Apple's reinvention through services and wearables, Netflix's pivot to global content, Tesla's shift towards energy and autonomy, and NVIDIA's evolution from gaming chips to powering the AI revolution — none of these inflections would have shown up in a standard five-year forecast. What looks expensive on next year's multiple often turns out to be wildly cheap over two decades. Terminal Value Investing breaks this trap by extending the forecasting lens and embedding qualitative drivers such as platform dynamics, reinvestment behaviour, founder intensity, pivots into new business models, and category creation into the valuation process. A short-term model may tell you what the business is. A long-term lens reveals what it's becoming.

The Quiet Power of Margin Expansion

While top-line growth dominates investor narratives, true wealth creation often happens behind the scenes, through the quiet, compounding power of margin expansion. In their early years, great companies can appear unremarkable. That's because they're channelling cash into growth engines: R&D, logistics, content, brand, or talent. Margins look weak. Profits are scarce. But that pain is strategic. As scale kicks in and network effects deepen, unit economics improve, fixed costs spread wider, pricing power strengthens, and digital flywheels accelerate.

Then the maths starts bending. Amazon moved from years of red ink to durable profitability, thanks largely to AWS. Netflix pushed its operating margin to over 20%. Tesla scaled to double-digit margins in an intensely competitive industry. When revenue growth meets rising profitability, the result is a nonlinear explosion in terminal value. Yet most investors and their models ignore this second engine entirely.

Five Ways Investors Miss the Climb

Even when they pick the right company, many investors fail to appreciate the shape of its journey. These are the most common errors:

1. **Sticker - Shock Valuation** – Dismissing a business for a high P/E without recognising tomorrow's optionality. (Apple in 2007)
2. **Static Margin Bias** – Assuming low margins will persist forever, even when scale leverage is imminent. (Amazon pre-AWS)
3. **Linear Extrapolation** – Projecting the past forward without anticipating inflection points. (Netflix's pivot to streaming)
4. **Reinvestment Myopia** – Interpreting heavy capex as weakness rather than strategic moat building. (Tesla before Model 3)
5. **Cultural Blindness** – Valuing only numbers while ignoring founder intensity, trust loops and customer cults. (Titan's retail flywheel, Infosys's client obsession)

Extending the Terminal Value Lens– A New Investment Framework

Terminal Value Investing demands a different toolkit, one that anticipates dynamic change rather than static continuation. Here's how it rethinks traditional assumptions:

Theme	Traditional Investor Mistake	Terminal Value Approach
Forecast Period	Assume 5–7 years then stagnation	Model 15–20 years of value-accretive growth
TAM Vision	Static view of market size	Anticipate new verticals and adjacencies
Margin Trajectory	Freeze today's margins	Model margin expansion via scale
Reinvestment Pain	Penalize early losses	Recognize them as moat-building efforts

Theme	Traditional Investor Mistake	Terminal Value Approach
Platform Thinking	Value single product	See gateway to monetization layers
Optionality	Ignore new business lines	Value latent, embedded options
Culture & Founder Edge	Undervalue resilience and DNA	Prioritize mission-driven intensity
Growth Assumption	Expect linear CAGR	Model for S-curves and resets
Volatility Response	Exit on noise	Endure turbulence with conviction

When multiple signals converge – a growing TAM, rising margins, founder grit, and reinvestment intensity – it's not the time to shrink your lens. It's time to stretch it.

Quick Filters for Spotting the Next Everest Climb

- Is the TAM still widening or about to?
- Are margins flat today but mechanically destined to rise with scale?
- What hidden options could unlock a second S-curve?
- Does leadership display founder intensity and cultural resilience?
- Is the reinvestment flywheel turning faster despite market impatience?

When several of those boxes light up, extend your valuation lens, because the visible ridgeline is only the base of the climb.

Investor Takeaways – What Most Models Miss

- Model in decades, not five-year slices: a five-year forecast tells the story, but a twenty-year horizon reveals the legend.
- Treat margin expansion as a second engine. Growth alone is powerful; growth plus leverage is exponential.

- Respect reinvestment pain. Near-term losses often signal moat construction, not weakness.
- Factor in culture and leadership. They are the hardest advantages to replicate and the easiest to ignore.
- Look for the hidden S-curve. Optionality, platforms and TAM resets are the real sources of 100-baggers.

The Everest climb happens beyond the visible ridgeline. Train your eyes to see past it.

PART III

ENDURANCE - THE INVESTOR'S MINDSET

CHAPTER 16

The Costliest Exit - Why Most Investors Sell Too Soon

"If the job has been correctly done when a common stock is purchased, the time to sell it is almost never."
— Philip Fisher, Common Stocks and Uncommon Profits (1958)

Investing legends are often remembered for their brilliant stock picks. But even the greatest minds have one thing in common: they have all regretted selling too soon. The real cost in Terminal Value Investing is not always in picking the wrong company; it is in exiting the right one before the compounding magic plays out.

This chapter revisits some of the most powerful and painful stories of early exits: Peter Lynch in Taco Bell, Carl Icahn in Netflix, Warren Buffett in Disney, Baillie Gifford in Amazon, and Sequoia Capital in Apple. These aren't tales of loss. They are tales of lost potential. And they carry timeless lessons on what it truly takes to capture a 100x return.

Carl Icahn & Netflix – A $2 Billion Win That Could Have Been $8 Billion

In October 2012, Netflix was reeling from its Qwikster blunder and investor scepticism. That's when Carl Icahn stepped in, quietly amassing a 10% stake at $58 per share (pre-split). He believed in Reed Hastings's vision and Netflix's first-mover advantage in streaming.

Within 14 months, the stock returned 457% and Icahn sold around half his stake in 2013, probably thinking it was reasonable and wanting to book profits. By 2015, he exited entirely at around $678 pre-split, realising a $2 billion gain. However, Netflix would go on to split 7-for-1, expand globally, and soar past $1200 post-split by mid-2025. Had he held, Icahn's position could have been worth over 100x the original value.

Howard Marks & Apple: Value Meets Platform Explosion

In one of the most common investor struggles: holding on to extraordinary compounders, he uses Apple as a case in point:

Today, another 10 years later, Apple is around $180, up 12x since 2013 and up by almost 500x since 2003. The point is, in the face of these gains, very few investors would still hold all they had originally bought.

Marks does not disclose exact entry or exit points in Apple, but his admission illustrates the difficulty of sticking with high performers through volatility and valuation anxiety. Investors like Marks, who are fundamentally grounded in value investing, often find it hard to reconcile rapid price appreciation with discipline, even when business momentum supports the thesis.

Had an early investor bought Apple in the early 2000s at under $1 (split-adjusted), and held through the launch of the iPhone (2007), App Store (2008), Apple Silicon (2020), and a services flywheel that now contributes nearly a quarter of its revenue, they would have seen the company evolve into a $3 trillion tech ecosystem. As of early September 2025, the stock trades around $230, over a 40x rise from its early smartphone era valuations.

The lesson, as Marks admits, is not just about buying right but staying invested when greatness is still compounding.

Peter Lynch & Taco Bell – The One That Got Bought Too Soon

In the early 1970s, Lynch started buying Taco Bell at around $7 per share. When the market crashed in 1973–74, the stock dropped to $1. Lynch held firm. The fundamentals – store expansion, no debt and unit profitability – remained strong.

By 1978, Taco Bell was the Magellan Fund's largest holding. That year, PepsiCo acquired it for $42 per share. A win? Yes. But Lynch always believed it cut short a generational compounding story. 'It would have gone to $400 if Pepsi hadn't bought it out,' he later said. Like McDonald's or Domino's, Taco Bell had optionality that never got realised independently.

Suze Orman's Amazon Exit: Great Instincts, Bitter Regret

Suze Orman is an American financial adviser, bestselling author, television host, and motivational speaker, widely recognised for her work in personal finance education. Known for her conservative approach to investing and her emphatic advocacy for financial discipline, Orman has helped millions of individuals navigate debt, savings, and retirement planning. But even the most seasoned voices can look back with regret.

In 1997, Orman bought shares of Amazon, simply because she liked the name. It was a whimsical decision, but an uncannily prescient one. As Amazon's business model gained traction in the early 2000s, the stock began its historic ascent. Yet, like many investors tempted by early profits, Orman exited far too soon. Though she made a modest gain, she later admitted she now feels "sick to her stomach" thinking about what those shares would be worth today.

The lesson is timeless: don't duck out early from game-changing companies. Orman, who rarely recommends buying individual stocks, now cautions that when you do invest in great businesses, it pays to hold on. Selling too soon, even at a profit, can turn into one of the most expensive mistakes an investor makes.

Warren Buffett & Disney – A 1,000x That Slipped Away

In 1966, Buffett bought 5% of Disney for $4 million (market valuation of less than $90 million) after meeting Walt Disney personally. At the time, Disney had just launched Mary Poppins and owned valuable content and land. He sold the stake for a 50% gain, a decision he later called a $10 billion mistake.

Had he held, that $4 million would be worth over $10 billion today, even excluding dividends.

Sequoia Capital & Apple – The One That Got Away

In 1977, Sequoia Capital invested $150,000 in a fledgling PC start-up called Apple. Just two years later, before Apple's landmark IPO in 1980, the firm exited its position for roughly $6 million. On paper, it was a 40x return. But in hindsight, it was a fraction of what could have been. Apple would go on to define the modern consumer tech era, and Sequoia had stepped off the rocket ship too soon.

Today, Apple is worth over $3 trillion, a level of value creation few could have imagined back then. The iPhone, App Store, Apple Silicon, and its rapidly growing services business turned Apple into a platform company with massive global reach. The iPhone alone catalysed an entirely new TAM, expanded margins, and deepened customer loyalty at a scale that rewrote what tech investing could mean.

The lesson was clear: selling early, even with a profit, can be costly when you back a generational company. Sequoia learnt this first-hand.

Chastened but wiser, the firm evolved. No longer content with just early-stage wins, Sequoia restructured its investment model to stay involved across a company's entire lifecycle, from seed rounds through IPO and beyond. The goal: never let a compounding miracle slip away again.

Yahoo's Alibaba Exit: The $100 Billion Regret

In 2005, Yahoo made one of the most lucrative early bets in tech history, investing $1 billion for a 40% stake in a little-known Chinese start-up: Alibaba. At the time, the Chinese e-commerce market was still nascent, and Jack Ma's vision appeared audacious. But as Alibaba's platform scaled rapidly through Taobao, Tmall, and Alipay, it became clear that Yahoo had stumbled upon a once-in-a-generation compounder.

Yet, driven by pressure to deliver near-term results and facing internal turmoil, Yahoo began unwinding its stake well before Alibaba's 2014 IPO. By then, the stake could have been worth over $100 billion, but much of that upside had already been left on the table. What could have transformed Yahoo's future instead became a footnote in its decline. The irony? The most valuable thing Yahoo ever owned wasn't even Yahoo — it was what they didn't hold on to.

Lesson: Corporate impatience and the pressure to 'show results' today often lead to exits that cost fortunes tomorrow.

Peter Thiel: IPO Liquidity vs Long-Term Upside

Peter Thiel's early investment in Facebook stands as one of Silicon Valley's most dramatic stories of exit regret. In 2004, Thiel invested just $500,000 in Facebook, transforming it into a 10% stake in Mark Zuckerberg's nascent company. By the time Facebook went public in May 2012, he held around 26 million shares. Shortly after the IPO and expiration of the lock-up period, Thiel sold approximately 80% of his stake, netting over $1 billion, about $640 million in the IPO and $396 million shortly thereafter.

At the time, this appeared astute: liquidity, diversification, and realisation of a phenomenal win. But in hindsight, it became painfully clear how much upside was sacrificed. Had Thiel held his stake, it would have grown to a value measured in tens of billions, given Facebook's rise into a trillion-dollar-plus enterprise.

Lesson: IPO liquidity often serves as the enemy of long-term compounding. The allure of a billion-dollar payday led Thiel to trim a stake that could have been worth 10× more if held.

SoftBank's Nvidia Stake: The $150 Billion Regret

In 2019, SoftBank's $100 billion Vision Fund held a 4.9% stake in Nvidia, acquired for roughly $700 million in 2017. By the time that stake was sold to 'lock in returns', it was worth about $3.3–3.6 billion, a tidy gain at the time that seemed prudent during a volatile period.

However, SoftBank's CEO Masayoshi Son later voiced deep regret, dubbing the stake "the fish that got away." He revealed that those shares would now be worth around $150–160 billion, leaving a staggering unrealised gain of over $150 billion on the table.

Lesson: The pressure for immediate performance and short-term liquidity, even in mega-compounders, can lead to exits that cost more than they earn. With Nvidia riding the AI wave post-2019, the decision remains one of corporate investing's most painful what-ifs.

Why Do Most Investors Sell Too Soon?

Anchoring to Entry Price - "I bought at ₹100, it's now ₹500. That's enough." But compounding has no memory. The business might just be getting started.

The Dopamine of Booking Gains - A win feels good. But locking in a 5× return might cost you the remaining 95×.

Valuation Anxiety – "It looks expensive." Amazon did too for 20 years.

Volatility Fatigue – 100x stocks drop 40–60% multiple times. Weak hands exit. Strong hands endure.

FOMO and Peer Pressure - Everyone else is rotating to the next hot thing. You follow. The compounding engine keeps running – without you.

Narrative Fatigue – When the story gets old, investors get bored. But the best businesses compound quietly.

Confirmation Bias – You start looking for reasons to sell. And of course, you find them.

Terminal Value Requires Terminal Patience

Investor Takeaways: The Patience Premium

- The greatest returns don't come in the thrill of early growth; they arrive silently, over decades of compounding that most investors never witness. Terminal Value Investing isn't just about identifying exceptional businesses. It's about resisting the urge to exit when the climb feels long and the summit unseen.
- The real risk isn't in holding too long; it's in selling just before exponential momentum kicks in. As the saying goes, most investors never miss the summit because it's too far, but because they turn back too soon.
- Reaching the Everest of investing takes more than vision; it demands stamina. The most extraordinary rewards lie not in the first leap, but in the long, uneventful stretch where conviction is tested and patience pays.

The Final Climb

On the journey to the summit, greatness rarely announces itself. It unfolds slowly, quietly, and often in defiance of short-term logic. The hardest part isn't spotting the potential. It's staying the course long enough to see it realised.

CHAPTER 17

The Patience Premium – Legendary Investors Who Let Time Do the Heavy Lifting

"The stock market is filled with individuals who know the price of everything, but the value of nothing."

— ***Philip A. Fisher***

Philip Fisher showed investors what kind of businesses to own. Warren Buffett revealed how long to own them. Together, they drew the blueprint for turning great companies into generational fortunes. The road to a 100-bagger rarely begins with a hot tip or a clever trade. It begins with vision, the ability to imagine a company two or three strategic moves ahead and the discipline to sit quietly while that vision plays out. Long before '100-bagger' entered the investment lexicon, a handful of practitioners were already letting capital, competitive advantage, and time do the compounding. Their track records remind us that the most valuable skill in markets is not predicting the next quarter, but refusing to interrupt a snowball once it has started to roll.

The eleven portraits that follow explore investors who each turned a single position into a hundredfold (or greater) gain. Their journeys reveal not only why they bought but, more importantly, why they stayed. From mid-century stock pickers to modern globalists, their examples provide enduring lessons on the art of patience.

Finding the right company is only half the battle. The harder half is holding on when every headline, market downdraft, or shiny new sector tempts you to sell. Century club investors share one defining trait: patience. Far from passivity, patience is an active decision, a willingness to endure volatility, to ignore the false urgency of quarterly earnings, and to trust in the long runway of an exceptional business. The greatest investors combined insight with endurance: they bought companies with expanding moats and reinvestment engines, then did something profoundly counterintuitive — they did nothing.

What follows is a series of stories spanning industries, geographies and decades. Each underscores the same truth: compounding is most powerful when left undisturbed.

The Rakesh Jhunjhunwala: A Masterclass in Patience

In 2001 Rakesh Jhunjhunwala met Titan's managers, studied its fledgling jewellery experiment and concluded the market was missing a generational shift. The stock, scarcely followed and priced at barely ₹2 (post-split basis), still looked like a sleepy watchmaker groping its way into India's unruly gold trade. Most investors would have taken a quick double and moved on; Jhunjhunwala instead focused on three intangibles — brand trust, an aspirational middle class and a management culture willing to reinvest patiently — and then did the hardest thing in investing: he waited.

Over the next two decades Titan endured currency crises, demand slumps, regulatory shocks and periodic 50-plus-per-cent drawdowns, yet it kept compounding, expanding from watches into jewellery, eyewear and fashion while deepening its nationwide retail moat. By 2025 the share price sat above ₹3,600, a gain of roughly 1,800-fold. The Titan saga is less a lesson in clever timing than in resolute ownership: spotting a durable franchise early, sizing up, and letting compounding, powered by culture and consumer tailwinds, work for twenty years.

Chuck Akre & American Tower: Compounding on Steel and Spectrum

In 2002, American Tower looked like anything but a future compounder. Laden with debt and branded with 'junk' credit ratings, it was written off by many investors as a busted roll-up from the telecoms boom. Chuck Akre, however, saw something different. He began buying shares at depressed levels, around $5, even as the stock plunged to under $1. What drew him in was a deceptively simple but profound insight: a mobile phone tower is like a toll bridge for the airwaves. Once the steel was in the ground, every additional tenant added to the tower brought incremental revenue at almost no cost, creating royalty-like economics.

As mobile data consumption exploded through the 2000s and 2010s, tenancy ratios climbed from just over 1 per tower to more than 2.5. Operating margins surged above 50%, cash flows compounded, and American Tower expanded globally into Latin America, Europe, Africa, and Asia. For Akre, this investment embodied his "three-legged stool" philosophy: high returns on invested capital, a long runway for reinvestment, and capable management. From those early purchases, American Tower delivered more than 100× returns, transforming from a distressed infrastructure play into one of the greatest compounders in modern US equity history.

Nick Sleep: Radical Patience and Time Arbitrage

Between 2001 and 2014, Nick Sleep's Nomad Investment Partnership quietly compounded 921%, outpacing many famed investors. His edge was not in trading brilliance but in an unusual discipline: radical patience. Sleep's philosophy of 'time arbitrage' meant focusing on what businesses could become in 10–20 years, while most investors obsessed over the next quarter.

Nomad's defining bets were on Amazon (2001) and Costco (2002). While critics balked at valuations and near-term losses, Sleep saw something deeper: both companies were building 'scale economies shared' – passing efficiencies back to customers, reinforcing loyalty, and widening moats. By the time he closed Nomad in 2014, Amazon had risen ~20× and Costco ~12×; those who held longer would eventually see them become full 100-baggers.

His letters emphasised customer surplus as the ultimate moat, far more enduring than accounting ratios. He endured brutal drawdowns by trusting that companies prioritising customer value would, over time, create immense shareholder value. As he wrote: 'Good work doesn't have to be frantic.'

In 2014, constrained by regulatory pressures, Sleep returned capital and urged investors to stay the course. He continued investing privately, free from quarterly scrutiny, under a simple mantra: 'Get rich – slow.' His legacy remains a masterclass in long-term compounding, showing how patience itself can be the most underrated edge in investing.

Philip Fisher & Motorola: A 45-Year Lesson in Let-It-Ride Investing

When Philip Fisher first visited Motorola's Chicago plant in 1955, the company was best known for car radios. What impressed him wasn't the gadgets, but the culture: engineers were given priority over accountants, R&D dominated the budget, and management openly discussed ten-year roadmaps. Fisher saw a company wired for reinvention. He began buying shares under $0.50 (split-adjusted) and never sold.

Over the next five decades, Motorola repeatedly reinvented itself, moving from car radios into defence electronics, semiconductors, pagers, and eventually the first generation of mass-market mobile phones. Revenues grew from $227 million in 1956 to $27 billion by 2004. Fisher simply sat tight. He often said the biggest returns come not from frantic trading but from 'sitting quietly' on businesses that keep improving. His Motorola stake proved the point: according to his estimates, $1,000 invested in 1957 became roughly $2 million by the late 1990s, a 2,000× return, or ~20% CAGR across four decades.

Fisher's Motorola journey remains a parable of true long-term investing. By identifying a culture of innovation and refusing to interrupt compounding, he turned a mid-century radio company into a half-century wealth engine. His lesson endures: when you find a business capable of compounding through reinvention, the hardest and smartest move is to wait.

Warren Buffett: The Oracle of Long Patience

Warren Buffett's genius lies less in predicting markets than in identifying enduring moats and then sitting patiently while compounding does the work. His career is built on a few cornerstone investments, each a study in the power of patience.

- **Coca-Cola: Brand, Sugar, and a River of Dividends**
  Coca-Cola showcases how patience multiplies a moat's economics without heroic reinvestment. An asset-light concentrate model, century-deep brand memory, and unrivalled distribution mean modest unit growth plus periodic pricing can sustain high returns on capital. By sitting still, Berkshire harvested growing cash pay-outs while avoiding taxes and frictions that frequent traders incur. KO proves that the premium for waiting is real: when the engine is durable, time, not activity, does the heavy lifting (numbers consolidated in Chapter 20).

- **American Express: From Crisis to Fintech Royalty**
  Buffett first bought American Express during the Salad Oil Scandal of 1964, investing $13 million when others fled. He built the stake further between 1998 and 2012. Today, Berkshire owns ~21.6% of AmEx, worth over $45 billion and yielding more than $400 million a year in dividends. For Buffett, AmEx exemplified how brand trust and network effects endure long after crises fade.
- **GEICO: Turning Insurance Float into an Equity Geyser**
  Berkshire's GEICO story began in 1976 with a $23.5M rescue ($4.1M common, the rest convertible preferred) and roughly $46M invested by 1980, taking the holdings to 33%. Buybacks through the '80s–mid-'90s lifted Berkshire to ~50%, and in 1996 it purchased the remaining 49% for about $2.3B, total cost over 1976–1996. GEICO's direct-to-consumer model keeps distribution costs structurally low, generating sizeable low-cost float that has financed other Berkshire bets. 'On 2024 results and 2025 run-rate, GEICO screens at roughly $75B of stand-alone value over 500x of its initial investments.'
- **See's Candies: A $25 Million Moat**
  In 1972, Berkshire acquired See's Candies for $25 million. The business has since generated more than $2 billion in pre-tax profits whilst requiring under $40 million in incremental capital. Its loyal customer base and pricing power illustrate Buffett's principle that the best businesses turn modest capital into rivers of cash without constant reinvestment.
- **Moody's: The Rating Monopoly**
  Spun off from Dun & Bradstreet, Moody's became a quiet powerhouse in Berkshire's portfolio. With regulatory moats and limited competition, it compounded steadily for decades, showing how network effects and barriers to entry can sustain dominance.

- **Apple: A Late but Defining Pivot**
  For decades Buffett avoided technology, but between 2016 and 2018 Berkshire invested approximately $35 billion in Apple. By 2023, the stake had grown to $173 billion, powered by Apple's sticky ecosystem, pricing power, and relentless share buybacks. It became Berkshire's largest holding, proof that Buffett could still pivot and compound capital late in his career.
- **BYD: The Chinese Wild Card**
  At Charlie Munger's urging, Berkshire invested $232 million in BYD in 2008, acquiring 225 million shares. Then a battery upstart, BYD has since grown into the world's number one EV maker, selling 3.7 million vehicles in 2024 and driving battery costs below $60/kWh. While Berkshire trimmed its position, it still owns over 5% worth approximately $8 billion, a 30× return. BYD now leads in both EVs and grid-scale energy storage, expanding into Europe and Southeast Asia.
- **Burlington Northern Santa Fe: Betting on America's Backbone**
  In 2009, during the aftermath of the financial crisis, Buffett spent $44 billion to acquire BNSF Railway outright. He called it an 'all-in wager on America'. The railroad has since become one of Berkshire's most reliable cash engines, producing steady, high-margin earnings across cycles.

The Pattern

Across these investments, a simple framework repeats:

- Enduring Moats: brand (Coke, See's), trust (AmEx, Moody's), cost advantage (GEICO, BYD), or network scale (Apple, BNSF).
- Self-Funding Growth: dividends, buybacks, or float recycle capital without dilution.

- Owner-Oriented Managers: leaders who widen the moat instead of empire-building.
- Patience: decades-long holding periods, enduring scandals, recessions, and volatility.

As Buffett famously put it: "Time is the friend of the wonderful business, the enemy of the mediocre." His true edge has been mathematical patience, buying cash-rich moats, keeping the tax meter idle, and letting time turn them into 100-baggers.

Peter Lynch: The Visionary of Everyday Investing

Peter Lynch, legendary manager of Fidelity's Magellan Fund from 1977 to 1990, turned a modest $18 million fund into $14 billion, compounding at 29.2% annually versus the S&P 500's 15.8%. His success wasn't built on complex models but on a deceptively simple idea: 'Invest in what you know.' He believed everyday observations – long lines at stores, popular products at home, shifting consumer tastes – gave ordinary investors an edge over Wall Street analysts.

Lynch's genius lay not just in spotting winners but in holding them through volatility and scepticism. He coined the term 'ten-baggers' for stocks that could rise tenfold, and Magellan owned dozens. A sighting of long queues at Dunkin' Donuts in 1979 led to a major purchase at $0.40 split-adjusted, eventually delivering 10 to 15×. Hanes became another winner after Lynch noticed his wife buying L'eggs pantyhose, an everyday product with massive scale potential. Perhaps his most telling story is Taco Bell, covered in Chapter 16.

Beyond stock-picking, Lynch preached temperament: "The real key to making money in stocks is not to get scared out of them." His books One Up on Wall Street and Beating the Street remain timeless guides, advocating deep research, rational expectations, and the courage to sit through the noise.

Lynch's enduring lesson is that the best ideas often hide in plain sight. For investors willing to trust their fieldwork, ignore short-term panic and let time do its work, everyday life can point the way to extraordinary fortunes.

Thomas Russo: The Global Compounding Purist

Thomas Russo, long-time partner at Gardner Russo & Quinn, has built his investing legacy around one elegant principle: "capacity to suffer." This philosophy reflects his preference for companies that are willing to forgo short-term profits to pursue long-term value creation. Russo champions global consumer franchises such as Nestlé, Heineken, LVMH, Pernod Ricard, Berkshire Hathaway, Mastercard, Alphabet, and Netflix, firms that reinvest aggressively in brand equity, marketing, distribution, and emerging markets, regardless of quarterly earnings optics.

Russo famously noted, "Capacity to suffer is the essential ingredient to compound wealth". His approach focuses not on GAAP-reported profits but on 'look-through earnings' – the long-term economic benefits accruing to shareholders. Overseeing more than $10 billion in assets, he values leaders who allocate capital with patience and discipline over decades. While others chase short-term earnings beats, Russo seeks what he calls 'quiet compounding' – the understated, yet powerful growth that emerges when brand power is combined with long-term reinvestment.

Li Lu: Backing the Electric Future with BYD

Li Lu, the quiet but deeply respected investor behind Himalaya Capital, found his long-term gem in BYD, China's electric vehicle and battery manufacturer. He first invested in 2008, well before EVs were considered mainstream. Buffett famously backed Li's conviction by purchasing a stake in BYD through Berkshire Hathaway. Over the years, Li Lu held steady as BYD navigated economic cycles, policy shifts and fierce competition. Today, BYD is not just an EV leader in China; it's a global force rivalling Tesla in many respects. Li Lu's patience in BYD showcases how foresight, aligned with a willingness to endure short-term pain, can yield extraordinary long-term rewards.

Ron Baron: Riding Tesla and SpaceX Through the Storms

Ron Baron, founder of Baron Capital, exemplifies the rare discipline of long-term conviction in growth investing. In 2014, when Tesla was widely dismissed as a hype-driven bet, Baron made a bold move, investing hundreds of millions of dollars. Ignoring market noise and volatility, he stayed focused on Tesla's mission, visionary leadership, and improving unit economics. That patience paid off: by 2023, Baron Capital's stake in Tesla had grown to over $6 billion, helping deliver a ~45% five-year CAGR in the Baron Partners Fund through 2021.

Beyond Tesla, Baron also invested more than $1 billion in SpaceX, calling it one of his most exciting long-term opportunities. Though privately held and not fully reflected in fund valuations, Baron projects that SpaceX could be worth $500 billion by 2030. As for Tesla, he has stated the company could reach a $1.5 to $2 trillion valuation in the next decade and even suggested it might scale as high as $5 trillion.

Baron's journey is a masterclass in conviction-led investing, tuning out short-term distractions, trusting deep research, and allowing compounding to work over time. His story shows that true long-term success often appears irrational at first, but it's precisely that foresight and patience that drives exceptional returns.

Charlie Munger: The Architecture of Patience

Charlie Munger, vice chairman of Berkshire Hathaway, built his wealth through deep conviction and lifelong patience. He began investing in Berkshire in the late 1960s and formally became vice chairman in 1978, holding nearly his entire net worth in the company for decades. Under his influence, Berkshire shifted from buying cheap stocks to acquiring high-quality businesses. From 1965 to 2024, Berkshire compounded at approximately 20% annually.

Munger also served on Costco's board from 1997 to 2021 and invested personally and via Daily Journal Corp. He viewed Costco as a fortress business, built on scale, loyalty, and price discipline. Even into his 90s, he declared that if he could own only one stock, it would be Costco. From 2000 to 2023, it compounded at approximately 16% annually.

Whether with Costco or Berkshire, Munger's greatest edge wasn't just intellect, it was patience. As he often said, "The big money is in the waiting."

Raamdeo Agrawal: Riding Patience with Hero Honda

In 1995–96, Raamdeo Agrawal bought Hero Honda shares at around ₹30, investing ₹10 lakh in what would become one of India's most iconic long-term investments. At the time, India's two-wheeler market was shifting from scooters to fuel-efficient motorcycles, and Hero Honda, with its reliable CD100 (Commuter Deluxe) and rural reach, was at the forefront of this transition.

Agrawal saw this structural shift early. He recognised the potential of a consumer-led mobility boom powered by affordability, trust, and a rising middle class. Hero Honda's "Fill it, shut it, forget it" campaign captured that moment, and so did Agrawal's conviction.

He held the stock for nearly 20 years, even through its 2010 split with Honda. By the time he exited around 2015–16, the stock had surged past ₹2,600, delivering over 86× capital gains, excluding dividends. Though he exited personally, Motilal Oswal's institutional funds continue to hold the stock — testament to his long-term thesis.

Agrawal's Hero Honda bet is a case study in marrying business quality with structural trends, and letting patience do the compounding.

It was the height of the dotcom boom, when non-IT stocks traded at deep discounts.

Investor Takeaways: The Test After Take-off

Insight	Why It Matters
The first 5× is hard. The next 20× is harder - because you'll want to sell.	Patience is most difficult when your gains already feel "enough."
Compounding works best when left alone.	Legendary investors didn't chase alpha - they let businesses do the heavy lifting.
The most painful volatility usually precedes the biggest gains.	Every journey involved storms, long plateaus, or sharp drawdowns.

Common Threads: The Legendary Club Checklist

- Entered early, often amid neglect, controversy, or scepticism
- Owned businesses with moats that deepened with scale like network effects, brand power, cost advantages
- Backed managements that reinvested at high incremental ROIC, even at the cost of near-term profits

- Held through crises, CEO changes, and product revolutions
- Practised a temperament of disciplined inactivity once the thesis was working

These stories prove that 10×, 100×, even 1,000× outcomes are not lottery wins. They are the compound interest of deep research, bold conviction, and an iron stomach. The formula is deceptively simple yet painfully difficult: buy a business where returns on capital improve with scale, get in before consensus, and resist every urge to sell. Time does the rest, as it did for Fisher, Buffett, and the quiet legends who followed them.

Timeless Traits of Legendary Investors

- Bought during crises or periods of neglect
- Held across multiple decades
- Backed visionary founders or enduring management teams
- Benefited from massive TAM expansion paired with disciplined reinvestment
- Ignored short-term volatility, focusing relentlessly on long-term business quality

Conclusion: Patience as the Final Edge

The greatest investors profiled in this chapter proved that the hardest part of compounding isn't finding the right business, it's staying with it once success begins. The urge to lock in gains can be overwhelming, especially when volatility punishes conviction. Yet patience is the true differentiator: it is what transforms a good investment into a generational fortune.

The climb to 100× is never linear. There are storms, false summits and long stretches of doubt. But those who stand their ground and refuse to interrupt the snowball once it's rolling are the ones who ultimately reach the summit.

In the chapters ahead, we'll take the final step: understanding why Terminal Value Investing delivers not only extraordinary returns but does so with greater consistency and durability than any other approach. That consistency is the enduring edge, the discipline and design that keep you at the summit long after others have turned back.

CHAPTER 18

The Enduring Edge - How Terminal Value Investing Outlasts All Others

"The strongest of all warriors are these two – Time and Patience."
— ***Leo Tolstoy, War and Peace***

In the climb to wealth, most strategies run out of breath. Terminal Value Investing just keeps ascending.

When investors discuss strategy, the debate often centres on "value versus growth" or "momentum versus fundamentals." Yet most of these approaches are geared towards near-term gains measured in months or a few years. Terminal Value Investing (TVI), by contrast, is built for the long haul. It focuses on capturing the full power of compounding over decades by honing in on a company's ability to reinvest its cash at high returns.

This chapter explains how Terminal Value Investing (TVI) stands apart, and why it can deliver 100× outcomes where other methods often fall short. We explore several prominent investment philosophies and show, through detailed cases and real-world examples, why the TVI approach is characterised by deep research, minimal turnover, and a focus on reinvestment quality. It is uniquely positioned to turn small stakes into Generational wealth.

The Major Investment Philosophies at a Glance

Investment Style	Core Focus	Time Horizon	Primary Goal	Typical Tools	Key Risk
Terminal Value Investing	Long-term cash flows & reinvestment capacity	10–30+ years	Maximize wealth via compounding and durability	DCF, ROIC, FCF, Moats, Business Quality	Selling too early or misjudging long-term moat
Value Investing	Undervalued assets (price < intrinsic value)	1–5 years	Mean reversion to fair value	P/E, P/B, Margin of Safety	Value traps; ignoring business deterioration
Growth Investing	Companies with high revenue/ earnings growth	3–7 years	Capitalize on high growth before maturity	Sales CAGR, TAM, Market share	Overpaying for growth; no path to profitability
Momentum Investing	Stocks with strong recent performance	Weeks to year	Ride short-term trends	Price action, volume, moving averages	Sudden reversals; no valuation anchor
Technical Investing	Chart patterns & price indicators	Intra-day to month	Predict short-term price movements	RSI, MACD, Candlestick patterns	False breakouts; no link to fundamentals
Concept Investing	Betting on new product categories/ tech	3–10 years	Anticipate future demand & category creation	Industry trends, early traction	Hype cycles, unproven models
Theme Investing	Broad macro or sectoral narratives	1–10 years	Capture secular shifts (e.g., EVs, fintech)	ETFs, sector screens, trend analysis	Picking the wrong theme or entering too late

Why These Approaches Often Fall Short of 100×

1. Value Investing
   Traditional value focuses on undervalued stocks relative to near-term metrics (P/E, P/B). It hopes for mean reversion to fair value.
   - Why it misses 100×: It shies away from high-quality compounders that look 'expensive' early on. If a company is reinvesting heavily for future growth, short-term earnings may look underwhelming or overpriced.
   - TVI difference: Rather than fixate on near-term multiples, TVI will pay fairly for a business whose reinvestment engine can span decades, allowing compounding to outstrip initial valuation concerns.
2. Growth Investing
   Growth investing involves buying companies with fast revenue or earnings expansion, aiming to profit before the market anticipates a plateau.
   - Why it misses 100×: Growth investors often sell once growth moderates, even if the business is still compounding cash flows over time.
   - TVI difference: TVI looks for sustainable, durable growth plus disciplined reinvestment. Even if the top line decelerates, a firm can keep compounding if it channels free cash into high-return projects.
3. Momentum Investing
   Momentum investing chases stocks with strong recent price action, assuming winners keep winning in the short to medium term.
   - Why it misses 100×: It is price-centric, typically exiting positions too soon. Momentum strategies rarely hold through multi-year drawdowns or expansions.

- TVI difference: TVI is business-centric, indifferent to short-term volatility. The focus is on how the company compounds internally, not how the stock trades externally.

4. Technical Investing

   Technical analysis uses charts, RSI, MACD, candlesticks, etc. to forecast near-term moves.

   - Why it misses 100×: It's purely about trading signals, ignoring fundamentals. Without an understanding of a company's moat or capital allocation, holding for a decade seldom happens.
   - TVI difference: TVI draws insights from cash flow sustainability, pricing power and ROIC. Short-term chart patterns have no bearing on multi-decade wealth creation.

5. Concept Investing

   Concept investors back bold, unproven ideas (like early EVs, AI, or genomics) on the premise that demand will follow.

   - Why it misses 100×: A high proportion of concept stocks fail due to poor execution, unproven models or capital starvation. Even winners often face dilution and hype crashes.
   - TVI difference: TVI can still invest in "big ideas," but demands evidence of a scalable moat and reinvestment runway. It's vision + discipline, not pure speculation.

6. Theme Investing

   Theme investors bet on broad narratives like clean energy, digitisation, or demographics.

   - Why it misses 100×: Even if the theme is correct, the basket approach often includes mediocre companies. Timing the theme is also tricky.
   - TVI difference: TVI identifies a single future category killer within that theme—one that can reinvest and expand for decades—rather than scattering capital across average players.

What Sets Terminal Value Investing Apart

1. **Multi-Decade Horizon**
   While most strategies aim for 1–5 years (value, growth) or even less (momentum, technical), TVI envisions 10–30 years. It captures the full lifecycle of compounding, from early expansions to global dominance.
2. **Conviction over Timing**
   TVI does not attempt to pick precise entries and exits based on news or chart signals. Instead, it bets on business durability and a consistent reinvestment engine. Price corrections are tolerated if the thesis remains intact.
3. **Reinvestment Focus**
   Many styles revolve around price or momentum. TVI is about what the company does with its capital—reinvesting at high ROIC, building moats that deepen over time.
4. **Low Activity, High Understanding**
   Momentum or technical investors might churn positions weekly. TVI calls for deep research and minimal turnover. It's about knowing a few great businesses intimately and letting them run.

The path to 100× often comes from a handful of extraordinary picks. TVI is comfortable with concentrated holdings that endure volatility and cycles. It's not about diversifying across 50 names; it's about truly understanding five or six.

Example in Practice: ASML (2015)

Consider ASML at ~$100 in 2015:

- Momentum investor: Buys on breakout news (e.g. EUV progress), sells on delays or lack of immediate follow-through.
- Concept investor: Likes the "future of chips" narrative but exits before scale is achieved.

- Theme investor: Bets on semiconductors broadly, spreading capital across chip designers and fabs, diluting exposure to ASML.
- Growth investor: Rides revenue spikes from new machine cycles but exits on cyclicality fears.
- Technical trader: Watches price channels and moving averages, missing the long-term monopoly forming.
- Value investor: Avoids ASML due to seemingly high multiples and R&D expense drag.

A Terminal Value Investor (TVI), however, asks:

If ASML becomes the sole supplier of EUV lithography to the world's most advanced chipmakers and continues reinvesting into deeper tech moats, what is its terminal value?

The TVI approach centres on the core business mechanics:

- Can ASML protect and expand its EUV monopoly?
- Will it sustain high ROIC through decades of chip innovation?
- Is it slowing down progress in Moore's Law, instead of just being one of the companies that help make chips?

With scale, margin expansion, and decades of EUV capex cycles ahead, ASML's long-term cash flows could far outweigh short-term earnings noise, turning a misunderstood R&D-heavy stock into a generational compounder.

They fixate on short- to medium-term performance.

- They do not hold through the inevitable drawdowns or cyclical slowdowns.
- They miss the power of relentless reinvestment and brand lock-in.

Common Threads: The Legendary-Club Checklist

- Early Entry During Neglect or Controversy
- Moats that widen with scale — network effects, brand loyalty, or cost leadership.
- Managements that reinvest at high incremental ROIC, often sacrificing short-term margins.
- Holding periods that span crises, CEO changes, even product revolutions.
- Temperament: a bias toward inactivity once the thesis is working.

These investors prove that 100-fold outcomes are not lottery wins; they are the compound interest on deep research, high conviction, and an iron stomach. Find the rare business where returns on capital improve with size, buy before everyone else believes, and then don't interrupt the compounding. Time will do the rest, just as it did for Fisher, Buffett, and the quiet legends who followed them.

Investor Takeaways - The Art of Doing Almost Nothing

Terminal Value Investing, by contrast, is engineered for enduring patience, compounding mathematics and the unwavering belief that if you own the right business, time is your greatest ally.

Terminal Value Investing isn't about catching every dip or riding every rally. It's about betting on a handful of exceptional companies, letting them grow, and most importantly, refusing to sell prematurely when the real wealth creation has only begun. Over 10, 20, even 30 years, a business's reinvestment ability can transform an initial stake into a 100× fortune. That is the essence of the Terminal Value approach: time, patience, and the high art of doing almost nothing.

PART IV

LEGACIES, CASE STUDIES & THE FINAL SUMMIT

CHAPTER

19 The Century Club – Where Arithmetic Becomes Alchemy

"Find a business that can compound at a high rate,
and then do the hardest thing in investing: hold on."
— ***Patrick O'Shaughnessy, Infinite Loops***

From Storytelling to Spreadsheets

Everyone envies a 100-bagger after the fact. Yet beneath every spectacular chart is a patient compounding engine which is fuelled by boring maths and uncommon conviction. Earlier chapters dissected the qualitative flywheels: TAM expansion, moat widening, margin lift, reinvestment discipline. Now we flip the lens to the quantitative backbone that quietly turns pocket change into dynastic wealth.

What Makes These Companies Special?

The Century Club isn't just a list of high performers. It's a pattern recognition exercise in strategic evolution, operational excellence, and relentless time in the game.

These companies didn't merely grow; they transformed. Some companies like Apple, Amazon, and Netflix didn't just ride secular tailwinds; they architected entirely new ecosystems. Others like Titan and Moutai stepped into chaotic, unorganised markets and imposed structure, trust, and scale where little existed before.

But transformation alone wasn't enough. These companies converted scale into profit. Their growth wasn't just about top-line momentum; it was also about leverage. Pricing power, operating discipline and category leadership turned expanding revenue into even faster-growing operating profits. Whether it was AWS quietly driving Amazon's margin shift or Royal Enfield reviving Eicher Motors, they found internal flywheels that compounded quietly and powerfully.

Most important of all, they endured. They compounded for decades, not quarters. Even NVIDIA, with the shortest timeline in the set, condensed a transformative cycle into nine explosive years. The rest – Infosys, HDFC Bank, Netflix, ASML, FICO and others – proved that compounding doesn't require fireworks, just flawless repetition in expanding arenas.

Their secret was not forecasting the future. It was building for it and holding the course long enough for the maths to show up.

The Three Unifying Traits:

1. They evolved. From products to platforms, and from noise to category leadership.
2. They scaled with discipline. Margins widened even as growth accelerated – proof of deepening moats.
3. They compounded patiently. The biggest gains came not from speed, but from staying power.

These aren't isolated success stories. They are case studies in compounding strategy, operating models that rewired industries over decades. What follows is not legend. It's maths in motion.

What the Numbers Really Say

In investing lore, '100-bagger' outcomes often feel mythical. But behind the magic lies maths and not luck. The Century Club is not a celebration of stock charts. It is a dissection of what happens when growth, margins and duration align.

To decode this, we analysed a curated group of 19 companies that grew their stock prices 100-fold or more over multi-decade periods. For each, we compared:

- Stock CAGR (price appreciation)
- Operating Profit (OP) Increase
- Sales CAGR, and
- Return Multiple

Together, these metrics are captured in two foundational tables:

Table 6: The Compounding Engines of the Century Club

100x Compounders: Return Multiples and CAGR

Company	Currency	Base Year	Base Year Price	Price August 2025	No of Years	Return Multiple	CAGR
Microsoft	$	Jun-86	0.11	520	39	4727	24%
Titan	₹	Mar-01	2.07	3499	24	1690	36%
Amazon	$	Dec-97	0.25	224	28	896	27%
HDFC Bank	₹	Mar-98	5.47	1993	27	364	24%
Apple	$	Sep-01	0.28	233	24	832	32%
Kweichow Moutai	RMB	Dec-02	6	1426	27	238	27%
Infosys	₹	Mar-98	8.9	1450	27	163	21%

Company	Currency	Base Year	Base Year Price	Price August 2025	No of Years	Return Multiple	CAGR
ASML	$	Dec-95	3.12	755	30	242	20%
NVIDIA	$	Jan-16	0.73	181	9	248	85%
AutoZone	$	Aug-95	26.88	4036	30	150	18%
Netflix	$	Dec-02	0.76	1204	23	1585	38%
Monster	$	Dec-02	0.04	64	23	1604	38%
Home Depot	$	Jan-85	0.36	407	40	1131	19%
Walmart	$	Jan-75	0.01	100	50	10000	20%
Ansys	$	Dec-00	2.81	336	25	120	21%
FICO	$	Sep-00	5.62	1355	25	241	25%
Eicher Motors	₹	Mar-08	24.18	5758	17	238	38%
Booking Holdings	$	Dec-00	7.9	5447	25	689	30%
Bajaj Finance	₹	Mar-10	3.1	857	15	276	45%

Table 7: The Century Club: Stock Price and Operating Profit CAGRs of 100x Compounders

Stock Performance Summary

Company	No of Years	Sales CAGR	OP Increase	Stock CAGR	Returns Multiple
Microsoft	39	20%	26%	24%	4727
Titan	24	20.9%	-1%	36%	1690
Amazon	27	36%	29%	27%	896
HDFC Bank	27	31%	-13%	24%	364
Apple	23	21%	38%	32%	832
Kweichow Moutai	23	24%	32%	27%	238
Infosys	27	27%	-4%	21%	163

ASML	29	14%	9%	20%	242
NVIDIA	9	43%	46%	85%	248
AutoZone	29	8.2%	8%	18%	150
Netflix	22	29%	34%	38%	1585
Monster	22	22%	20%	38%	1604
Home Depot	40	16%	-1%	19%	1131
Walmart	50	17%	-1%	20%	10000
Ansys	24	16%	2%	21%	120
FICO	24	8%	31%	25%	241
Eicher Motors	17	28%	29%	38%	238
Booking Holdings	24	13%	58%	30%	689
Bajaj Finance	15	33%	17%	45%	276

Highlights from the Century Club Dataset

The tables present a rare breed of businesses, those that have multiplied shareholder wealth 100× or more, often over multi-decade horizons. The compounding maths behind these returns offers timeless lessons for investors focused on long-term wealth creation.

Super Compounders: Growth + Time = Explosive Returns

Some companies achieved staggering stock price CAGRs by combining high revenue growth with expanding profit margins:

- **NVIDIA** (2016–2025) is the standout performer, compounding at 85% annually over just nine years. This was driven by a blistering 43% sales CAGR and 46% OPM expansion, reflecting its rise as a core enabler of AI and high-performance computing.

- **Netflix** and **Monster Beverage** delivered **38**% stock CAGRs over 22 years, riding massive behavioural and category shifts, streaming for Netflix and energy drinks for Monster. Netflix and Monster expanded operating profit margins by approximately 34% and 20% respectively, signalling strong internal economics, not just top-line hype.
- **Amazon** grew sales at a 36% CAGR**,** expanded operating margins by 29 percentage points, and delivered a 27% stock CAGR over 27 years, a textbook case of how growth plus time creates explosive compounding.
- **Bajaj Finance** (2010–2025) achieved a 45% stock CAGR over 15 years, backed by a 33% sales CAGR and strong, steady profitability, showcasing reinvestment at scale in a fast-formalising Indian credit market.
- **Apple** (2001–2024) compounded at 32%, with a stunning 38% expansion in operating profit margin and 21% revenue CAGR, epitomising the power of ecosystem economics and monetising hardware + services.

These are the true ‘compounding engines’, companies that not only grew rapidly but also deepened their economic moats.

Margin-Led Multipliers: When Profits Outpace Sales

Some businesses turned modest sales growth into big shareholder value through margin expansion and capital efficiency:

- **FICO** (2000–2024) achieved 25% stock CAGR with only 8% sales growth, thanks to a 31% operating profit margin expansion. This reflects a pricing-power model with sticky analytics and expanding SaaS margins.
- **Booking Holdings** (2000–2024) turned 13% revenue CAGR into 30% stock CAGR, largely driven by 58% operating profit

margin expansion. It's a case of margin leverage and asset-light scale in online travel.

- **Kweichow Moutai** compounded at 27%, with a robust 33% OPM expansion, confirming how brand prestige and pricing power create long-term optionality in luxury consumer staples.

Slow and Steady Titans: Time Is the Ultimate Multiplier

Even without blistering growth rates, some companies delivered massive return multiples by simply sustaining mid-teens CAGRs over long periods:

- **Walmart** compounded at 20% over 50 years, turning $1 into $10,000. This underscores the value of dominating a vast TAM with execution consistency.
- **Home Depot** posted a 19% CAGR for 40 years, built on category leadership, scale and disciplined reinvestment in retail infrastructure.
- **Microsoft**, despite being founded in 1975 and going public in 1986, delivered 24% CAGR over 39 years, showing that even tech giants can keep compounding if they evolve (e.g. Office to Azure).

These cases highlight that you don't always need hypergrowth; what you need is enduring relevance and operational resilience.

Growth Without Profit Expansion: Valuation and Optionality Matter

Some compounders achieved extraordinary stock returns despite flat or declining operating margins, highlighting the role of market leadership, rerating and optionality:

- **Titan** compounded at 36% CAGR even though operating profit margin declined slightly (−1%). The stock re-rated as the company formalised India's jewellery sector and built deep consumer trust.

- **HDFC Bank** delivered 24% CAGR with a -13% change in PBT, suggesting that capital efficiency, loan book quality and brand strength mattered more than short-term margin trends.
- **Infosys** also showed this pattern: strong top-line growth with subdued or negative OPM shifts, yet the stock still compounded at over 20%, thanks to secular demand and platform transition tailwinds.

Mid-Cap Marvels: Category Creators with Focus

Some companies created or reshaped niche markets with focused strategies and branding:

- **Eicher Motors** turned Royal Enfield into a premium biking icon in India, delivering 38% CAGR with 28% sales and 29% PBT expansion. It built aspiration where none existed.
- **Ansys** and **AutoZone** showed how niche focus, in simulation software and auto parts retail, can produce consistent double-digit compounding with lower volatility.

Meta-Lessons from the Dataset

- **There's no single formula for 100×.** Some companies grew by scaling revenue; others by expanding margins or reinvesting wisely. A few did all three.
- **Duration matters as much as velocity.** Walmart, Microsoft, and Home Depot proved that a 15–20% Sales CAGR held over 30–50 years can deliver 100× or even 1000× in stock returns.
- **Margins, Moats, and Markets must align.** The biggest winners nailed at least two out of three, and the truly great ones managed all three.

- **Early optionality often looks inefficient.** Companies like Netflix spent years reinvesting or transitioning their business models before compounding showed up in earnings.

Five Enduring Patterns Behind 100x Compounders

1. **Tiny Beginnings, Towering Outcomes**
   Most 100× journeys began in obscurity. Microsoft at $0.11, Apple at $0.28, Titan at ₹2.07, Netflix at $0.76 (all adjusted for splits and bonuses) – these weren't blue chips; they were rounding errors. What they lacked in scale, they compensated for with runway. A small base meant that even incremental progress compounded exponentially. These companies didn't need to be big to begin with; they needed the ability to grow, adapt and scale for decades.
2. **Time Is the Ultimate Multiplier**
   While some businesses raced ahead with blazing speed, like NVIDIA and Bajaj Finance, others took the scenic route. Walmart, Home Depot, and Microsoft showed that compounding at even 18–24% for 30–50 years can turn a modest investment into a life-altering outcome. The dataset reinforces a timeless truth: 25% CAGR sustained for 25 years yields over 250×. It wasn't superior forecasting that unlocked wealth; it was the discipline to stay invested. Time didn't just heal volatility; it magnified quality.
3. **Profits Pull the Stock Forward**
   In the long arc of compounding, stock prices tend to follow the trajectory of operating profits. Across the dataset, companies with the strongest return multiples, such as Apple, Netflix, Monster and FICO, also posted the most impressive OPM growth. The correlation between stock CAGR and operating profit growth was strong and consistent. This wasn't luck; it was cash flow compounding in action. Short-term narratives fade, but profit engines leave lasting footprints in price charts.

4. **Valuation Worries Fade, Fundamentals Endure**
   Amazon and Netflix were long labelled 'overvalued'. Critics pointed to their sky-high P/E ratios and warned of bubbles. But as each company scaled and expanded margins, those early fears dissolved. In hindsight, their multiples didn't compress; they were earned. When growth is profitable, durable and self-reinforcing, valuation anxiety becomes noise. The market eventually catches up to the business, not the other way round.
5. **Moats Are Forged, Not Found**
   Most of these compounders didn't start with defensibility baked in; they built it along the way. FICO's scoring models grew stronger with each data cycle. AutoZone scaled logistics, Titan won trust in jewellery, and Moutai ascended into a cultural symbol. These companies didn't rest on their edges; they sharpened them continuously. In a world obsessed with disruption, the real edge was quiet, cumulative, and hard to replicate.

Final Takeaway

The Century Club proves that great investing isn't about predicting quarterly beats, it's about recognising compounding machines early and holding them through storms.

In the end, every 100× story is a maths problem disguised as a patience test.

Hold the right mountain long enough, and arithmetic becomes alchemy – turning ordinary capital into extraordinary wealth.

CHAPTER

20

The Greatest Sip of All Time - One Share. One Century. $28 Million.

The Coca-Cola Story That Redefined Compounding

"The first rule of compounding: Never interrupt it unnecessarily."
— ***Charlie Munger***

Coca-Cola on 5 September 1919 quietly listed on the NYSE at $40 per share, issuing roughly 600,000 shares and valuing itself near $24 million, backed by a syrup formula, a curvy logo and a dream. That first year, the company generated $32 million in revenue and approximately a 9% margin, hardly the stuff of investing legends. But had you purchased just one share and reinvested every dividend along the way, your modest $40 outlay would have compounded into nearly 400,000 shares by mid-2025, valued at approximately $28.4 million. That's not a typo; it's a ~700,000× return, driven by a century of stock splits, dividend hikes and relentless reinvestment. *(As computed by ChatGPT Deep Research)*

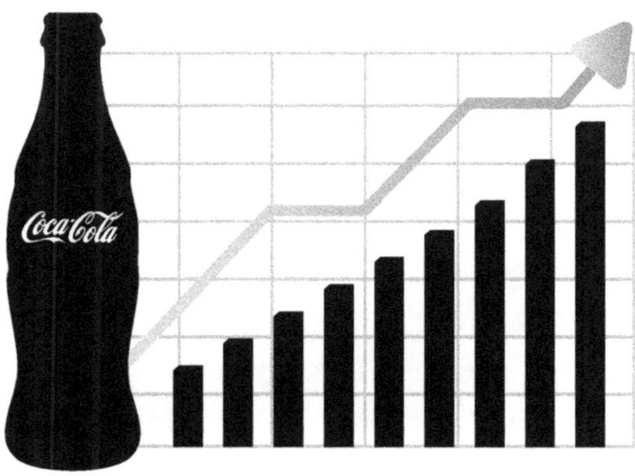

COCA-COLA: THE CENTURY-LONG MASTERCLASS IN COMPOUNDING

This transformation wasn't powered by speculation or timing the market; it was built on the back of discipline and the quiet miracle of compounding. With 10 splits turning one share into 9,216, and every dividend reinvested, including fractional shares, the position swelled over time. Coca-Cola has raised its dividend for 63 consecutive years, making each pay-out not just income but fuel for more growth. At $1.64 dividend per share in 2025, that's $656,000 annually in dividends – more than 16,000× the original investment every year. If ever there was a case for patience, reinvestment, and brand longevity, Coca-Cola is it.

The $40 Miracle: Coca-Cola (1919–2025)

Metric	Value
Initial Investment	$40 (1 share in 1919)
Final Share Count	~400,000 shares
Share Price (June 2025)	~$71
Total Value	~$28.4 million
2025 Annual Dividend Income	~$656,000
Total Return Multiple	~693,000×
Implied CAGR (105¾ years)	~13.6–14.1%

Coca-Cola: The War-Time Flywheel

The Coca-Cola flywheel began spinning in the 1920s, when president Robert Woodruff pushed innovations such as the six-pack carrier, which tripled at-home consumption by making it easier for families to buy multiple bottles at once. This period marked the start of Coca-Cola's transition from a refreshment to a daily staple, embedding the brand into everyday American life. By the eve of the Second World War, Coca-Cola had already mastered the art of franchised bottling and nationwide distribution.

The flywheel shifted into overdrive during World War II, when Woodruff declared that every U.S. soldier should be able to buy a Coke for a nickel, 'wherever he is and whatever it costs the Company.' Backed by the War Department, Coca-Cola was allowed to classify its syrup as 'essential' for troop morale, and it installed 64 portable bottling plants across Europe, Africa, and the Pacific. By the time the war ended, this infrastructure became an instant global footprint, laying the groundwork for Coca-Cola's dominance. By the 1950s, the company's asset-light concentrate model was exporting syrup to every continent, making its red-and-white script one of the most recognised symbols in the world.

Coca-Cola – Product Breadth Marches in Lockstep

Across the decades, Coca-Cola's brand momentum wasn't just about incremental growth; it was fuelled by consistent product innovation. During the 1940s, Fanta was created under wartime constraints using locally sourced ingredients in Germany, exemplifying creativity born of necessity. In the early 1960s, Coca-Cola introduced Sprite to compete in the lemon-lime space. Juice diversification followed as the company adopted Minute Maid, originally founded in 1945 and acquired by Coca-Cola in 1960, to become its flagship juice concentrate.

The 1980s marked a pivotal shift when Diet Coke debuted in 1982 and quickly rose to become the number one diet soft drink in the US within its first year. By the end of 1984, it had surged to become the third-largest soft drink in the country, behind only Coke and Pepsi.

In the ensuing decades, Coca-Cola significantly broadened its portfolio: Coke Zero, Powerade, and Dasani shaped its beverage evolution in the 2000s. More recently, their acquisitions and stakes, such as Costa Coffee, Fairlife Milk, Topo Chico Hard Seltzer, and a 16.7% stake in Monster Energy, demonstrate Coca-Cola's ambition to dominate every beverage occasion without eroding the essence of its core brands.

Buffett & Coca-Cola: The $1 Billion Sip That Never Ended

Warren Buffett stamped the ultimate seal of approval when Berkshire bought 6.2% of the company in 1988 for about $1 billion; he has never sold a share and now collects over $700 million in annual dividends on that position. Ten stock splits since IPO mean one original share equals 9,216 shares today, while the dividend has risen for 63 consecutive years. Those two levers, split multiplication and reinvested cash, explain how total shareholder return far outstripped the ≈ 12,500× jump in market capitalisation from $24 million to ≈ $300 billion.

Modern numbers still fizz: $47 billion in revenue and a 21% GAAP operating margin in 2024, 2 billion servings poured daily across 200 countries and brand equity valued above $60 billion. A share trades near $70, and the company remains a Dividend King with six-plus decades of raises.

Investor Takeaways – When Brand Meets Time

Coca-Cola pairs an emotional moat (brand love) with a structural moat (asset-light bottling economics) and seizes every inflection point, from the WWII 'nickel Coke' pledge to Diet Coke, Buffett's endorsement, and the Monster alliance. Give that model a century and even the smallest sip of equity compounds into generational wealth – proof that time really is the friend of a wonderful company.

CHAPTER

21 Lesson from History - 1991: The Year India Unlocked Terminal Growth

"No power on earth can stop an idea whose time has come."
— ***Dr Manmohan Singh, Finance Minister of India, Budget Speech, 1991*** (Singh quoted French romantic novelist Victor Hugo in his speech).

Every great compounding journey begins with a structural unlock. For India, that moment was 1991. In the early 1990s, India was still trudging along at what economists called the 'Hindu Rate of Growth', a modest 3 – 4% annually. The economy was shackled by the Licence Raj, foreign exchange controls, import restrictions, and public sector dominance. For decades, this low-growth environment placed a natural ceiling on business potential and investor expectations.

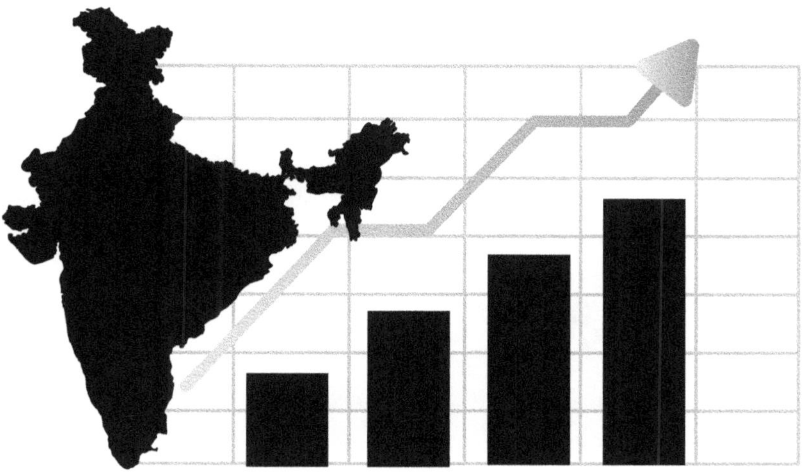

EVERY NATION'S EVEREST BEGINS WITH ONE BOLD STEP — 1991 WAS INDIA'S

That changed dramatically in 1991.

Faced with a severe balance of payments crisis, India was on the brink of default. In response, newly appointed Finance Minister Dr Manmohan Singh, under Prime Minister P.V. Narasimha Rao, unveiled a sweeping set of economic reforms that liberalised the Indian economy.

Key reforms included:

- Dismantling of the License Raj
- Opening of the economy to foreign direct investment
- Liberalisation of trade and tariffs
- Privatisation of state-run enterprises
- Financial Sector Reform and Capital Market Modernisation

This wasn't just a policy pivot, it was a structural reset. For the first time, Indian businesses could dream beyond domestic constraints. Export markets opened up. Capital became more accessible. The private sector gained room to compete and grow.

The Stock Market Reacts

In the one-year period between mid-1991 and mid-1992, the Indian stock market boomed, with the Sensex more than doubling in value. While some of this frenzy was later attributed to the Harshad Mehta securities scam, the truth remains that liberalisation marked the birth of modern Indian capitalism.

It was a turning point when the market began to reprice Indian companies, not just based on current earnings, but on future potential.

Investor Takeaways - 1991: When the Runway Doubled

This is what a true inflection point in terminal value looks like. The liberalisation of 1991 expanded India's long-term growth runway from a real 3% to 4% ceiling to 6% to 8% real growth rate and beyond. The Sensex was around 1300 in June 1991 and has risen to over 83000 as of June 2025, a CAGR of around 13%. It laid the foundation for multi-decade compounders like:

- Infosys (founded just before liberalisation, scaled after)
- HDFC Bank
- Titan, which thrived in the new consumer-driven India

Lesson: Policy Can Reshape the Playing Field

Great investors don't just follow companies; they understand when macro reform meets micro execution. The 1991 reforms did not change every business overnight, but they changed what was possible.

CHAPTER

22 Legacy Builders: Founders and Leaders Who Thought in Decades

"We never think in quarters. We think in decades."

— ***Narayana Murthy, Founder of Infosys***

Quarterly thinkers ride waves. Decade thinkers shape oceans.

Climbing Everest doesn't just require stamina; it requires vision. You don't summit a 29,000-foot peak by reacting to every gust of wind. You do it by studying terrain, planning for altitude, preparing for storms, and pacing for the long haul. Terminal Value Investing works the same way. It rewards those who back leaders not for next quarter's commentary, but for their ability to navigate tectonic shifts and to stay the course over decades.

This chapter profiles those rare founders and stewards who didn't just scale businesses; they scaled time. They weren't obsessed with quarterly optics; they were obsessed with vision, scale, and impact. They identified gaps before others saw them, moved early, built enduring teams, and shaped organisations capable of compounding far beyond their own leadership.

While leadership is central, it is not formally defined as one of the Four Pillars, Market Size, Moats, Reinvestment, and Patience because it is ultimately intangible. Leadership cannot be quantified with the same precision as market size or margins; it reveals itself only through decisions, culture, and long-term outcomes. Yet, it functions as the invisible force that holds the pillars together. Without visionary leadership, even the strongest market or moat can crumble; with it, ordinary resources can compound into extraordinary dynasties.

These are the decade-thinkers, quietly relentless, often misunderstood in the moment, whose choices compounded into legacies that outlasted business cycles and competitors alike.

Jeff Bezos: The Architect of the Infinite Flywheel

Bezos didn't start Amazon to sell books. He built a self-reinforcing loop of customer obsession, convenience and scale. From a bookstore to global commerce to logistics and warehousing to Prime Video to AWS, every reinvested dollar deepened Amazon's moat. His legendary 1997–2015 shareholder letters remain a masterclass in long-term thinking.

Legacy-defining impact: Codified the 'Day 1' culture and a customer-obsessed flywheel that continually broadens Amazon's moat, spanning retail, cloud, media, and even space.

Warren Buffett: The Oracle of Durability

Buffett's brilliance: not the purchase, but the long, disciplined hold on quality businesses through thick and thin. He turned Berkshire Hathaway into a compounding machine by focusing on capital efficiency, float leverage, and management trust. His favourite holding period? 'Forever.'

Legacy-defining impact: Proved that owning high-moat businesses indefinitely, financed by low-cost insurance float, can turn disciplined patience into multi-generational compounding.

Elon Musk: The Relentless First-Principles Builder

From PayPal's digital payments to Tesla's electric cars, SpaceX's reusable rockets, and Starlink's satellite internet, Elon Musk has built a career around making the 'impossible' possible. He relies on first-principles thinking, builds in-house when suppliers fall short, and sets bold timelines that rally talent and capital. Tesla forced the automotive industry to embrace electrification, scaling from the Roadster to mass-market models and building a global battery supply chain, while even opening patents to accelerate adoption. SpaceX cut launch costs dramatically with reusable Falcons and extended its advantage with Starlink's growing satellite network.

Legacy - defining impact: Musk normalised electric mobility and reusable rocketry, showing that bold vision, rapid iteration and personal risk-taking can reshape entire industries.

Bernard Arnault: The Keeper of Timelessness

Arnault didn't invent luxury; he institutionalised its mystique: at LVMH he systematically acquired heritage houses like Louis Vuitton, Dior, and Dom Pérignon, safeguarded their artistic soul, and scaled them with almost monastic discipline. In an era obsessed with disruption, he doubled down on permanence, craftsmanship, scarcity, and timeless design, treating every Maison as a cultural artefact rather than a product line. By vertically integrating supply chains, tightly controlling retail, and resisting overexposure, Arnault preserved each brand's aura even while expanding it worldwide. The result is a transformation of luxury from fashion to fortress: LVMH has become a 'temple of desirability', compounding demand through aspiration and inheritance. Where rivals chased trends, Arnault optimised for time, proving that when timelessness is managed with rigour, it becomes the most enduring moat of all.

Legacy-defining impact: Institutionalised timeless luxury by uniting heritage brands under disciplined scarcity and vertical integration, turning LVMH into a fortress where desire compounds across generations.

Narayana Murthy: The Outsourcing Visionary

Narayana Murthy was among the first, in the early 1980s, to see that software would become a global service and that India's deep engineering talent could power the world's back office. In 1981, armed with just ₹10,000 and a tiny Bangalore apartment, he co-founded Infosys on that insight, positioning the firm not as a low-cost code shop but as a high-trust technology partner. By embedding governance, transparency and meritocracy as strategic moats, Murthy fused visionary outsourcing with ethical rigour, turning Infosys into the bellwether of India's IT revolution and proving that values-rooted capitalism can scale to global relevance.

Legacy-defining impact: Pioneered trusted, ethics-first global IT outsourcing — elevating India from code factory to strategic technology partner.

Satya Nadella: The Culture Reformer

When Satya Nadella took Microsoft's helm in 2014, the once-dominant giant felt dated, anchored in Windows and Office, lagging in cloud, mobile and innovation. Nadella replaced the "Windows everywhere" doctrine with an "Azure everywhere" future, making cloud and AI Microsoft's growth engine. Equally vital, he dissolved silos, championed a growth mindset and infused empathy and lifelong learning into the company's DNA, triggering one of the most dramatic corporate revivals on record: revenues, profits and relevance soared as Microsoft reclaimed foundational status in enterprise tech.

Legacy-defining impact: Reoriented Microsoft around Azure and a learning culture, turning a mature incumbent into a cloud-and-AI powerhouse.

Bob Iger: The Strategist of Storytelling

Stepping in as Disney's CEO in 2005, Bob Iger wagered that timeless IP, not sheer content volume, would rule media's future. He executed a landmark acquisition spree — Pixar, Marvel, Lucasfilm, and 21st Century Fox — expanding Disney's constellation of beloved characters and story worlds. Iger then fused films, parks, merchandise, and streaming into a single flywheel, culminating in Disney+ (2019), which let the company own both narrative and distribution.

Legacy-defining impact: Assembled and integrated iconic IP into a direct-to-consumer ecosystem, turning Disney storytelling into a self-compounding global franchise machine.

Jensen Huang: The Relentless Parallel Thinker

Convinced that the future of computing was parallel, Huang spent two decades transforming GPUs from gaming chips into a new architecture for high-performance computing. His decade-long CUDA bet made GPUs programmable, so when deep learning exploded, NVIDIA's mature software stack, dominant hardware, and vast developer ecosystem were waiting. By 2025, the company had become the backbone of AI, robotics, autonomous vehicles, and data-centre compute.

Legacy-defining impact: Turned a niche graphics firm into the indispensable platform powering the global AI economy.

Sanjeev Bajaj: Architect of India's Consumer-Credit Revolution

Taking charge of Bajaj Finance, Bajaj shifted a modest vehicle-finance subsidiary into a lean, tech-first platform that democratised credit for millions of Indian consumers and SMEs. Early bets on EMI cards, consumer-durables financing, branch-light distribution, and data-driven underwriting lifted AUM at >35% CAGR and built a flywheel of cross-sell and customer stickiness.

Legacy-defining impact: Created India's most admired NBFC by pairing precision risk models with scalable, inclusive digital lending.

Wang Chuanfu: The Chemist Who Electrified the Future

Starting with low-cost rechargeable batteries in 1995, Wang vertically integrated BYD's entire supply chain, from raw materials to final packs, and then made the audacious pivot to EVs. Anticipating urban pollution and oil dependence, he pursued a dual track of electric buses and mass-market passenger cars, whilst investing heavily in R&D and domestic supply security. Today, BYD outsells Tesla in China and exports across Europe, Latin America, and SE Asia.

Legacy-defining impact: Built the industrial backbone for an electrified, self-reliant mobility future decades ahead of consensus.

Sam Walton: The Small-Town Merchant Who Redefined Retail

With one Rogers, Arkansas, store in 1962, Walton championed everyday-low pricing, rigorous cost control and rural focus, turning underserved small towns into a national advantage. He decentralised decisions, empowered front-line staff and invested early in distribution centres and satellite inventory systems, forging a logistics moat that scaled Walmart into America's largest retailer by 1992.

Legacy-defining impact: Proved that frugality, operational efficiency and customer service can compound to global retail dominance, where scale remains a servant, not a tyrant.

Larry Ellison: The Database Emperor

Larry Ellison didn't just build a company; he architected the infrastructure of enterprise software. Oracle became the backbone of corporate IT through a formidable combination of IP-rich databases, recurring revenue from long-term licensing, and near-impenetrable switching costs. As rivals chased user interfaces and consumer buzz, Ellison focused on control – that of data, systems, and architecture. Strategic acquisitions like PeopleSoft, Siebel, and Sun Microsystems broadened Oracle's empire across the full tech stack. The result: a backend giant with a market cap surpassing $600 billion. Ellison's brilliance wasn't in chasing the spotlight but in quietly owning the stage.

Legacy-defining impact: Embedded Oracle databases deep inside enterprise IT and expanded vertically to create a near-impenetrable software fortress.

Deepak Parekh: The Institution Builder

In a sector riddled with complexity and trust deficits, Deepak Parekh built HDFC into the gold standard of Indian finance. His focus on clean lending, risk management, and customer-first culture gave millions of Indians their first home and gave investors a front-row seat to decades of compounding. Parekh understood that institutions aren't made by ambition alone; they require credibility, systems, and service. Long before fintech made headlines, HDFC quietly scaled both trust and returns. His genius lay in making boring beautiful and valuable.

Legacy-defining impact: Made HDFC India's trust benchmark by uniting disciplined risk with customer-centric lending, proving that "boring" finance can compound into a national institution.

Dhirubhai Ambani: Architect of Scale, Symbol of Aspiration

From a petrol-station attendant in Aden to launching Reliance in 1966, Dhirubhai Ambani bet on vertical integration and national self-reliance, moving from textiles to polyester, petrochemicals, refining, pipelines and, later, telecoms and retail. He spotted secular demand early, tapped India's public markets to democratise wealth, and built infrastructure that served the country as much as his company.

Legacy-defining impact: Proved that audacious scale, backward integration and public-shareholder capitalism could turn an emerging-market firm into a template for national ambition.

Sunil Bharti Mittal: Telecom Trailblazer

Starting with generators and push-button phones, Mittal secured a telecom licence in 1995 when India's teledensity was in single digits, outsourced network operations to global majors, and raced Airtel across the nation, then into Africa, whilst investing early in broadband and 4G. When Jio's price war erupted, Airtel raised capital, cut costs and bounced back, showing strategic agility.

Legacy-defining impact: Connected over a billion people by pairing asset-light outsourcing with bold spectrum bets, creating a resilient, pan-continental telecoms powerhouse.

Ingvar Kamprad: Democrat of Design

Launching IKEA at age 17, Kamprad re-engineered furniture economics with flat-packs, self-service warehouses, in-house design and relentless cost-consciousness. A mission-driven, privately held foundation structure keeps IKEA's values intact as it operates in 60+ countries.

Legacy-defining impact: Made good design affordable worldwide through system-level innovation and frugal culture, proving that values-led scale can endure for generations.

Amancio Ortega: Fast Fashion's Reluctant Billionaire

Beginning as a Galician shirtmaker, Ortega built Zara around speed and feedback, compressing design-to-shelf cycles to weeks. By keeping production close to Spain/Portugal, investing in logistics over advertising, and using store data as a real-time trend sensor, Inditex scaled to 7,000+ stores and leapfrogged GAP and H&M.

Legacy-defining impact: Turned fast fashion into an operating system, where rapid feedback, localised production and supply-chain mastery compound faster than style trends themselves.

Bill Gates: Architect of the Software Century

Gates grasped early that software, not hardware, would power computing's future, and he famously struck gold by licensing MS-DOS to IBM while retaining the rights, ensuring Microsoft earned a fee on every PC that flooded the market. That deal financed Windows, which soon dominated desktops worldwide. By bundling Word, Excel, PowerPoint, and Outlook, he created a productivity suite that scaled from homes to Fortune 500s, while deep investments in .NET, SQL Server, Visual Studio, Exchange, SharePoint, and early cloud built a full-stack enterprise footprint. Relentless R&D and platform thinking, not one-off products, kept Microsoft compounding long after Gates stepped down as CEO in 2000.

Legacy-defining impact: Built an interoperable, ubiquitous software architecture whose flywheel still powers the global digital economy.

Steve Jobs: The Perfectionist Who Made Technology Beautiful

Jobs fused hardware, software, and services into seamless experiences. The Macintosh set the design bar, the iPod married music to mobility, and the iPhone plus App Store turned Apple from product maker to ecosystem giant. His obsession with intuitive interfaces, tight vertical control, disciplined SKUs, and brand minimalism forged rabid customer loyalty and enviable margins. Developers flocked, users locked in, and Apple's integrated platform became a self-reinforcing moat.

Legacy-defining impact: Elevated technology into an emotionally resonant ecosystem, proving that design-led platforms can compound value and devotion long after the visionary is gone.

John Bogle: Democratizer of Wealth:

In 1976 Bogle launched the first index fund, ridiculed then as "Bogle's folly", and paired it with a client-owned Vanguard structure that rebates every cost saving to investors. He preached long-term, low-fee compounding and railed publicly against Wall Street's fee drag, eventually redirecting trillions into passive funds. Index funds now account for most U.S. domestic-equity fund assets. Vanguard's actively managed fixed-income funds and ETFs charge an asset-weighted average of *0.10%* (industry: *0.53%*); further, *2025* fee reductions alone are projected to save clients *$350 million+* this year.

Legacy-defining impact: Proved that broad-market indexing and investor-owned governance could outcompete high-cost active management, securing retirements for millions.

Howard Schultz: Brewing Culture at Scale

After a Milan espresso epiphany, Schultz bought Starbucks (then 11 stores) and recast it as a "third place" where baristas know your name, beans are ethically sourced, and playlists set the mood. He extended employee stock, healthcare and tuition, turning 400,000 "partners" into brand stewards and guided global expansion without losing café warmth. Starbucks now serves 100 million weekly guests across 80 countries, its mobile app a top US payments tool.

Legacy-defining impact: Transformed ordinary coffee into a cherished "third-place" ritual, proving that values-driven retail, founded on ethical sourcing, partner ownership and consistent in-store rituals, can command premium prices and daily loyalty.

Ray Kroc: Master of Scale and System

At 52, Ray Kroc stumbled upon a small California burger stand and saw not just a kitchen, but a scalable system. He franchised it with military discipline, standardised fry times, identical décor, and even counters designed at child height. To strengthen control, he created Franchise Realty Corp., purchasing land and leasing it back to operators, ensuring steady cash flow whilst keeping McDonald's asset-light. Soon, the golden arches were rising on every continent, serving 70 million meals daily.

Legacy-defining impact: Kroc fused process discipline with real estate leverage to build a fast-food empire that endured across tastes, recessions and generations.

Jim Sinegal: Frugal Genius of Wholesale Trust

Sinegal's Costco keeps only ~3,700 SKUs (vs 31,795 at a supermarket), caps mark-ups at 14%, and forgoes advertising, letting word-of-mouth and $65 memberships drive traffic. Employees earn industry-leading wages, reducing turnover and keeping floor expertise high. The result: revenue per square foot beats luxury retailers whilst customer satisfaction rivals Apple.

Legacy-defining impact: Showed that relentless value sharing with shoppers and staff can outcompound high-margin rivals in retail.

Phil Knight: Building Identity Through Performance

From selling Japanese running shoes out of his boot, Knight co-created the Swoosh, invested in Nike Air, and partnered with sports icons, from Jordan to Serena, to fuse athletic performance with cultural storytelling. He built Asia-centric supply chains for scale and funnelled marketing pounds into signature moments that made trainers fashion. Direct-to-consumer apps now give Nike data loops and premium margins.

Legacy-defining impact: Merged sport, tech and culture into a brand flywheel where inspiration and innovation feed each other worldwide.

Enzo Ferrari: Engineering Desire, Not Just Speed

A former Alfa Romeo racer, Ferrari founded Scuderia Ferrari for racing glory, then sold road cars only to fund the track. By capping production below demand, he kept waiting lists long, margins >25%, and brand mystique intact. Formula 1 victories reinforce showroom prices; bespoke paint and tailor-made interiors deepen emotional pull.

Legacy-defining impact: Harnessed scarcity plus motorsport pedigree to create a luxury brand whose value compounds on aspiration, not volume.

Leonardo Del Vecchio: Invisible Eyewear Emperor

Starting with metal frame parts in a Milan workshop, Del Vecchio acquired Ray-Ban, Oakley, LensCrafters, and Sunglass Hut, then merged with Essilor to own lenses too, controlling manufacturing, brands, retail, and even insurance. Most designer frames, from Prada to Chanel, are quietly produced under Luxottica licences.

Legacy-defining impact: Built a near-monopoly by vertically integrating the entire vision-care chain, turning everyday sight into a high-margin, globally defended business.

Hans Wilsdorf: Custodian of Horological Permanence

Wilsdorf's Rolex innovations – the waterproof Oyster, self-winding Perpetual rotor, and Datejust – made wristwatches rugged status symbols. In 1945 he placed Rolex into a foundation, shielding it from quarterly pressures and enabling deliberate under-production that keeps resale prices strong. Marketing feats – Everest ascents, deep-sea dives – linked technical trust with milestone moments.

Legacy-defining impact: Secured brand longevity by pairing engineering breakthroughs with mission-protected governance and intentional scarcity.

Marc Benioff: Champion of Cloud and Conscience

Declaring "no software," Benioff launched Salesforce as the first enterprise SaaS, then opened AppExchange to third-party developers, creating a CRM platform with network effects. Acquisitions like MuleSoft, Tableau, and Slack broadened its integration, analytics, and collaboration stack. His 1-1-1 pledge hard-wired philanthropy into corporate DNA, inspiring hundreds of companies to follow.

Legacy-defining impact: Proved cloud platforms and stakeholder capitalism can scale together, making purpose a competitive edge.

Reed Hastings: Architect of On-Demand Entertainment

After mailing DVDs to avoid late fees, Hastings bet Netflix's future on streaming in 2007, invested in recommendation algorithms, and greenlit originals like House of Cards, creating a binge model that upended release schedules. Today Netflix serves 300 million members in 190 countries, spends about $18 billion yearly on content, and measures success in minutes watched, not box-office weekends.

Legacy-defining impact: Redefined media by aligning technology, data, and storytelling into a self-funding global content fly-wheel.

Chuck Schwab: Broker for Main Street

Post-1975 deregulation, Schwab launched a discount brokerage with phone representatives open 24/7, later pioneering no-load mutual funds and zero-commission trades. Early online platforms made investing click-simple; the firm now custodies $8 trillion in client assets.

Legacy-defining impact: Tore down cost and access barriers, turning everyday savers into long-term investors.

Ken Langone: Merchant Who Empowered the Masses

Ken Langone raised Home Depot's seed capital and helped cement a culture where orange-apron associates deliver expert advice and share in equity. High-turnover, warehouse-style stores and a bias for owning the real estate threw off cash to fund a nationwide rollout. Today the chain sells about $150 billion a year and owns roughly 89% of its stores.

Legacy-defining impact: Demonstrated that financing, culture and customer empowerment can scale DIY retail into an enduring juggernaut.

Murali Divi: Silent Chemist of Global APIs

Shunning splashy generics, Divi's Laboratories specialised in complex APIs and custom synthesis, funding FDA-compliant mega-plants from retained earnings. Zero debt, 30%+ margins, and long-term contracts with Big Pharma turned a ₹10,000 start into a $20 billion giant.

Legacy-defining impact: Showed that precision chemistry, compliance and patient reinvestment can quietly build a world-leading pharmaceutical backend.

Investor Takeaways: Legacy Is the Longest Moat

Building a business is like climbing Everest; it takes more than ambition to reach the summit. It requires vision, patience, endurance and, above all, leadership that sees beyond the next ridge. The founders and CEOs in this chapter weren't just summiting earnings targets; they were mapping routes no one had climbed before.

They weren't just operators. They were architects of altitude.

Where others looked for exits, they planned base camps. Where markets saw peaks, they saw the summit line.

Terminal Value Investing flourishes in the hands of such decade-thinkers. No spreadsheet can capture the compounding force of belief sustained over decades. These leaders didn't just build companies. They left behind moats carved by time.

"Time is the most powerful moat. And legacy is its proof."

CHAPTER

23 The Summit: How to Recognise It, and What to Do

"He who climbs upon the highest mountains laughs at all tragedies, real or imaginary."

— ***Friedrich Nietzsche***

Most investors dream of the summit. Few know how to behave when they get there. In mountaineering and in investing, reaching the summit is not the end of the journey. It's a moment of perspective. Terminal Value Investing is built around the idea of identifying long compounding journeys. But even great businesses, over time, mature. The Total Addressable Market (TAM) gets saturated, reinvestment slows, and growth becomes harder to generate. That's the summit.

THE VIEW FROM THE SUMMIT IS BEAUTIFUL, BUT COMPOUNDING HAPPENS ON THE WAY UP.

The real challenge isn't just getting there. It's knowing what to do when you arrive.

What Is the Summit in Investing?

In Terminal Value Investing, the summit is the point where the climb changes. Growth that once felt effortless now demands every ounce of discipline. Companies that scaled on expansion must pivot to endurance, protecting margins, preserving cash flow and reinventing to stay relevant. It's not about share price or market cap; it's about reaching structural altitude.

The signs feel like thin air on a mountain:

- The market ahead looks narrower – TAM is close to tapped out.
- Each new step (reinvestment) yields less progress – ROIC falls.
- Breathing gets harder – margins flatten or compress.
- The pace slows – revenue growth decelerates.
- Climbers shed weight – Capex and R&D taper.
- Energy is rationed – cash is returned through dividends and buybacks.
- The wind turns – moats erode as competitors, regulators, or disruptors close in.

The summit is not failure, it is maturity. The view is magnificent, but the compounding ascent is behind you. The earlier an investor senses the thinning air, the wiser their next move will be.

What to Do When You Reach the Summit

Like mountaineers, investors don't live at the summit. Once there, three rational paths emerge:

Hold for Stability

If the company still delivers strong cash flows and maintains brand or pricing power, for instance Coca - Cola, it can still compound at a slower rate. This is wealth preservation and not aggressive wealth creation.

Exit Gracefully

If the market still values the company on past performance, but forward returns look muted, consider selling into strength. Exit while the narrative still holds, before earnings growth erodes conviction.

Reallocate to the Next Base Camp

Take the gains and reinvest in businesses still in the early stages of their terminal value journey, where TAM is expanding, moats are deepening and reinvestment is still high. It's not abandoning the climb; it's beginning the next one.

Emotional Biases That Cloud Judgment

The summit tests not just your logic, but your emotional discipline.

- Nostalgia Bias: This stock made me rich — how can I let go now?
- Identity Attachment: A long winner becomes more than a holding; it becomes personal.
- Recency Bias: Assuming past CAGR continues indefinitely.
- Fear of Regret: Worrying that it may still have some upside left.

The lesson is simple: the summit demands rationality over sentiment. Knowing when to exit is not a betrayal; it's wisdom.

Case Studies for The Summit

Coca-Cola: Holding for Stability

By the 1990s, Coca-Cola had reached the summit of global beverages. With markets across the world already saturated, revenue growth began to slow, and reinvestment opportunities grew scarce. Margins plateaued, and the company increasingly directed capital towards dividends and share buybacks rather than expansion. The signals were clear: slowing volume growth, higher payout ratios, and limited innovation beyond product extensions. For investors, Coca-Cola became the textbook case of "hold for stability". The business continues to generate strong cash flows, anchored by its brand power and pricing resilience, but its days as a high-growth compounder are long gone. Shareholders today benefit less from explosive compounding and more from steady dividends and defensive wealth preservation.

Infosys: From Hypergrowth to Stability

Infosys became the face of India's rise in global IT services. Through the 1990s and 2000s, it compounded revenues at over 30% annually, pioneering the offshore outsourcing model and scaling enterprise software and consulting engagements for Fortune 500 clients. By the mid-2010s, however, the summit was clear. The outsourcing TAM had matured, revenue growth slowed from the heady days of 30%+ to the mid-teens, and more recently to single digits. Leadership churn underscored the company's transition from a hypergrowth compounder to a mature cash generator. Today, Infosys remains financially strong, with robust returns on capital and 5–8% growth, but its golden era of exponential compounding has passed. The summit for Infosys marked a shift from aggressive wealth creation to dependable wealth preservation.

Intel: Summit and Moat Erosion

For two decades, Intel was the undisputed giant of semiconductors. Its 'Intel Inside' dominance gave it overwhelming market share in PC processors, monopoly-like margins, and massive free cash flows. By the 2010s, however, the PC market had matured, Moore's Law was slowing, and Intel failed to seize the mobile and smartphone opportunity. Competitors like AMD, Nvidia, and TSMC began outpacing Intel in innovation and execution. What had seemed like an impregnable moat eroded rapidly. Intel today remains only marginally profitable and is struggling to regain its former dominance, a stark reminder that even the strongest moats can erode when reinvestment falls behind and disruption accelerates.

IBM: Exit Gracefully Missed

IBM was once the backbone of global computing, reaching its summit in the 1980s and 1990s. Yet a pivotal decision to licence Microsoft's DOS rather than own the operating system shifted the economics of the PC era away from IBM. Over time, hardware commoditised whilst software and platforms accrued the lion's share of value. By the 2000s, revenue growth had stalled, margins compressed, and capital allocation leaned heavily on dividends and buybacks. Efforts to pivot into services, cloud, and analytics were slow and insufficient. Investors who failed to exit at the summit were left with decades of stagnation. IBM's story underscores the importance of recognising structural inflections early and selling into strength.

Procter & Gamble: Stability at the Summit

Procter & Gamble built a global empire of consumer staples with iconic brands like Tide, Pampers, and Gillette. For decades it was a reliable compounder, growing steadily as its products became household essentials worldwide. By the 2000s, however, TAM saturation in developed markets and rising competition made further expansion difficult. Revenue growth slowed, margins plateaued, and shareholder returns increasingly came from dividends and buybacks rather than reinvestment. Unlike IBM, P&G managed its summit with prudence, retaining stability and cash generation even as growth declined or slowed. For investors, the summit in P&G meant not collapse but a transition to wealth preservation and dependable dividends.

Nestlé: The Plateau of a Global Giant

Nestlé became the largest food company in the world, with iconic products spanning coffee, dairy, and packaged foods. Its rise was fuelled by brand strength, unmatched scale, and emerging market expansion. By the mid-2010s, however, Nestlé began to show the signs of maturity. Growth slowed to negligible levels as developed markets saturated, bottled water and packaged food categories faced competition, and reinvestment opportunities diminished. The company leaned on operational efficiencies and shareholder payouts to sustain returns. Nestlé's summit resembles Coca-Cola's: still a formidable global franchise with strong cash flows, but one whose best years of compounding are firmly in the past.

Cisco: The Dot-Com Summit

Cisco was the quintessential pick-and-shovel winner of the internet boom, dominating routers and networking equipment as the backbone of the web. Its market cap soared to over $500 billion during the dot-com era, when investors assumed its growth would continue indefinitely. But once the networking TAM matured after the bubble burst, revenues slowed and margins compressed. Despite steady acquisitions and diversification, Cisco never regained its hyper-growth trajectory. Today it is still a valuable, cash-generative company, but far removed from its summit years. Cisco's story highlights how technology cycles can propel companies to the peak, only for the plateau to arrive far sooner than expected.

Apple: Managing the Summit with Reinvention

Apple's meteoric climb was defined by the iPhone, which became one of the most successful products in business history. By 2015–2017, however, signs of the summit were visible: smartphone markets were saturated, unit growth had plateaued, and dependence on a single product created vulnerability. Many feared Apple's best years were over. Instead of fading, Apple managed the summit by reinventing its growth engines. Services such as the App Store, Apple Music, iCloud, and Apple Pay expanded its ecosystem, while wearables like the Apple Watch and AirPods opened new categories. Growth is slower today than during the iPhone's peak years, but Apple continues to generate extraordinary cash flows, combining stability with disciplined reinvention. Its journey shows that reaching the summit does not always mean decline; if managed well, it can be a platform for longevity.

The Spectrum of Summit Outcomes

These case studies highlight the different paths companies take once they reach the summit. Some settle into stable plateaus, others face erosion or collapse, a few stagnate when investors fail to exit, and rare exceptions reinvent themselves for a new climb. Together, they capture the full spectrum of outcomes when growth gives way to maturity, from the stability of household staples to the reinvention of tech giants.

- **Stable plateau:** Procter & Gamble, Nestlé, and Coca-Cola each transitioned into dependable, cash-rich franchises. Their golden compounding years are behind them, but they remain durable wealth-preservation machines, rewarding shareholders with steady dividends and defensive stability.

- **Erosion and disruption:** Intel and Cisco, where once-impenetrable moats weakened as reinvestment lagged and competitors surged.
- **Failure to exit:** IBM, where investors who clung on past maturity endured decades of stagnation.
- **Collapse:** General Electric, which went from the world's most valuable company to a cautionary tale of overreach and complexity.
- **Mature stability:** Infosys, which slowed from hypergrowth to steady but unspectacular compounding as India's IT outsourcing market matured.
- **Reinvention at the summit:** Apple, which faced smartphone saturation yet managed to expand into services and wearables, extending its longevity and proving that a summit can sometimes be a platform for renewal.

The Hardest Move: Selling a Winner

The hardest decision in investing is not buying early but exiting after a long, successful hold. Terminal Value Investors are trained to endure volatility, yet they must also learn to recognise stagnation. Holding a compounder through its golden years is wisdom; holding it through slow decline is complacency. Capital, like oxygen, must circulate. When it no longer fuels growth, it must find fresh air.

Investor Takeaways: The View from the Summit

Every summit offers a breathtaking view, not only of what has been gained, but also of what lies ahead. The greatest investors understand not just how to climb, but how to descend. They know when to pause, when to preserve, and when to prepare for the next ascent. The summit is not the end of compounding; it is a vantage point. From here, the investor surveys the horizon, ready to begin the next climb, wiser, higher, and with clearer perspective.

CHAPTER

24

When Terminal Value Becomes a Mirage

"The four most dangerous words in investing are:
'This time it's different.'"

— Sir John Templeton

Even great stories, when stretched too far, become myths. And myths make for dangerous investments. Terminal Value Investing rests on a powerful idea that certain exceptional companies, guided by deep moats and durable reinvestment models, can compound for decades. But not all mountains lead to summits. Some plateaus flatten. Others collapse. The Everest of Investing is not just about spotting climbers – it is also about knowing when the oxygen is running out.

The Mirage of Moats

Moats decay. They aren't forever. Technologies evolve, consumer tastes shift, and once impenetrable fortresses can fall into irrelevance.

BlackBerry: Moat Without Evolution

BlackBerry once controlled over 40% of the U.S. smartphone market. Its physical keyboard and enterprise-grade security were unmatched. Yet, when the world moved towards touchscreens and app ecosystems, BlackBerry stood still. Its moat, once admired, became obsolete.

Kodak: Killed by Its Own Invention

Kodak invented the digital camera in 1975 and then shelved it. Protecting its film profits became a strategic coffin. The moat it guarded so fiercely became the very wall that stopped it from evolving.

Nokia: Scale Without Platform

Nokia had global scale, design excellence, and decades of experience. But its loyalty to the Symbian OS, and its slowness to embrace touch and app ecosystems, proved fatal. Apple didn't just innovate; it redefined the category.

Investor Insight: If the core advantage no longer matters in the next paradigm, Terminal Value has already begun to erode.

Yahoo: User Base Without Product Vision

Yahoo was once the front page of the internet. But it missed every major wave: search (Google), social (Facebook), video (YouTube), messaging (WhatsApp). Its TAM wasn't just shrinking; it was fleeing. Even great execution cannot defy gravity when the market disappears beneath your feet. Yahoo lacked product cohesion. It tried to be everything – news, mail, ads, social – and ended up being nothing. Every reinvention diluted its brand and confused its users.

Investor Insight: Watch for loss of narrative clarity. Too many pivots often signal a loss of strategic soul.

Jet Airways: Brand Without Efficiency

Jet Airways was a pioneer in Indian aviation. Yet as lean, aggressive rivals like IndiGo optimised for cost and scale, Jet failed to adapt. A large TAM alone means nothing if you're not fit to climb it.

WeWork: TAM Without Viability

WeWork raised billions to reinvent office space. But its unit economics were broken from day one, leasing long-term and renting short-term. Add vanity side projects like WeGrow and wave pools, and the entire thesis collapsed under self-inflicted excess.

eBay: Network Effects Without Innovation

eBay, once a monopoly in online auctions, failed to reinvest in logistics, UX and ecosystem stickiness. Meanwhile, Amazon turned delivery into a moat. eBay stagnated as the world moved on.

Investor Insight: Reinvestment isn't always value-creating. Ask: is capital deepening the moat or expanding TAM? Or is it just being burned?

Vision Drift: When Strategy Becomes Noise

A strong business model often starts with focus. It ends with distraction.

Terminal Value Mirage: Summary Checklist

Signal	What to Watch For
Moat Decay	Customer churn, competitive parity, regulator hits
TAM Contraction	Declining category relevance, market migration
Capital Misallocation	Poor M&A, side ventures, bloated spending
Broken Unit Economics	CAC > LTV, margin compression, usage drop-off
Vision Drift	Strategic sprawl, brand dilution, focus lost

Investor Takeaways - Terminal Value Is Earned, Not Assumed

Every investor dreams of finding the next Amazon, Netflix or Infosys. But few see the risks hiding behind shiny narratives. A great story isn't enough; it needs staying power.

"Terminal Value isn't a forecast. It's an earned reality."

In the Everest of Investing, the real danger isn't missing the summit, it's mistaking a mirage for one. The best investors not only know what to climb... they know when it's time to descend.

CHAPTER

25

The Life Cycle of a Terminal Value Stock

"It's not the strongest of the species that survive, nor the most intelligent, but the one most responsive to change."

— ***Charles Darwin***

Every legendary wealth-creating stock has a lifecycle, a distinct journey from obscurity to dominance. Terminal Value Investing is about recognising not just what a business is today, but what it can become across time. By understanding the lifecycle of a terminal value stock, investors can better judge when to back it, when to be patient, and when to let go.

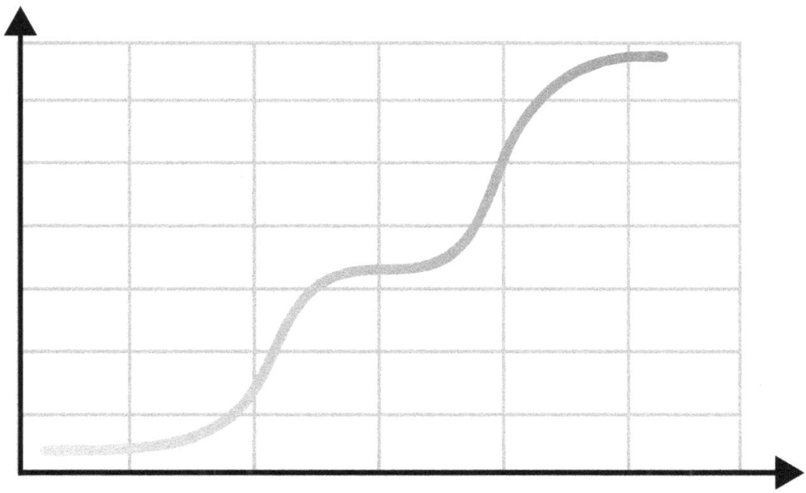

EVERY GREAT STOCK CLIMBS IN S-CURVES — THE LEGENDS START A SECOND ONE

1. Base Camp: The Spark of Potential

The journey begins at Base Camp, the origin stage where the company is often an unknown player solving a niche problem. At this stage, financials typically appear weak: revenues are modest, profits may be negative, and cash burn is common. But beneath the surface, there are signs of latent greatness, such as a rapidly expanding Total Addressable Market (TAM), a unique product, or a founding team with missionary zeal. Investors must look beyond ratios and search for early indicators of product-market fit, customer love, and long-term vision. Amazon and Infosys in the late 1990s and Apple in the early 2000s exemplify this stage. They looked unimpressive by conventional metrics, but held the DNA of future giants.

2. Ascent: Product Market Fit and Scaling

Once the product gains traction and demand accelerates, the company enters its Ascent phase. This is the climb from base camp to scale. Revenues begin to grow sharply, margins stabilise, and repeatable business begins to form. The company typically reinvests heavily into talent, distribution, infrastructure, technology, or brand to deepen its moat. Operating leverage may not be visible yet, as every surplus dollar is often redeployed to capture market share. But signs of compounding begin to emerge: increasing average revenue per user (ARPU), improving retention, and early pricing power. Optionality surfaces as new adjacent revenue streams come into view. For Terminal Value investors, this is the stage to hold firmly or even add, understanding that reinvestment, not short-term profitability, drives long-term returns.

3. Reinvestment Maturity: The Sweet Spot of Compounding

As a company reinvests successfully over time, it eventually enters Reinvestment Maturity, the phase where growth and profitability align. At this stage, the business benefits from scale efficiencies, a reinforced competitive moat, and a finely tuned operating engine. Margins expand, returns on capital improve, and cash flows become both strong and sustainable.

What makes this phase especially powerful is that the company not only generates more free cash flow than it needs, but still manages to deploy capital into meaningful growth opportunities. It's the golden era of compounding, where patience truly begins to pay off.

A classic example is Apple after the iPod and iPhone revolution. Investors who stayed the course through earlier volatility were rewarded with years of accelerating returns built on a foundation of deep reinvestment and scale.

4. Plateau: Maturity Without Decay

Eventually, the business enters a Plateau, a stage of maturity where growth begins to taper. Not because the company is failing, but because it has largely saturated its addressable market. Capital allocation begins to shift towards dividends, buybacks, or acquisitions. The business becomes more stable but less dynamic. Analyst coverage peaks, and market expectations normalise. This stage tests investor discipline. If the company continues to generate high returns on capital with minimal reinvestment needs in their later years, it can remain a valuable hold. But the days of explosive compounding are likely behind.

5. The Fork: Exit or Renewal

Every terminal value stock eventually reaches a Fork; this is a critical juncture that separates enduring compounders from fading giants. This is the point at which the business has likely exhausted its first S-curve of growth. *(An S-curve is a graphical representation of how a business or any growth process typically evolves over time. It gets its name from its shape: the curve starts slowly, accelerates sharply, and then flattens out, forming an 'S'.)*

The Total Addressable Market may be saturated, margins may have peaked, and incremental reinvestment no longer delivers the same return on capital.

At this stage, the question for investors is not what the company has achieved, but what it can achieve next. Can it identify and scale a new S-curve of growth, or will it slide into slow decline?

The S-curve, by nature, has three phases:

1. Early investment and effort with little visible output
2. Rapid, exponential compounding as scale kicks in
3. Flattening and tapering as growth slows and saturation sets in

Exceptional companies don't stop at one. They stack S-curves, transitioning from one growth engine to the next through bold reinvestment and strategic pivoting.

Take Microsoft. After decades of dominance in operating systems and productivity software, its growth plateaued in the early 2010s. Windows and Office were mature. Critics dismissed it as a 'has-been'. But under Satya Nadella, Microsoft launched a second S-curve, Azure and enterprise cloud**.** It reinvested billions into infrastructure, developer ecosystems, and hybrid cloud solutions. That pivot didn't just revive Microsoft, it catapulted it to over $3.5 trillion+ company, proving the power of reinvention at scale.

Similarly, Nvidia began as a gaming GPU company. It could have plateaued. Instead, it boldly bet on AI, high-performance computing

(HPC), and data centres, transforming its chip architecture and software stack (CUDA) to serve the future of machine learning. That second S-Curve – AI infrastructure – became its next Everest, delivering astronomical returns for long-term shareholders.

But not every company makes the turn. Many stall here. They engage in defensive M&A, over-diversify into low ROCE segments, or fail to inspire their next wave of internal innovation. Their culture ages. Capital is misallocated. ROCE declines. Moats erode.

This is the danger of the terminal value trap, when investors continue to hold based on past greatness, even though the reinvestment engine has shut down.

For the Terminal Value Investor, the fork is a moment of clear reckoning. If the company is launching a credible second S-curve, then back it. If not, exit rationally, without sentiment.

Investor Takeaways – Timing the Climb

Every great compounder follows a journey, and knowing the S-curve can help you stay the course. Many investors exit too soon at Base Camp, lose faith during the steep Margin Ascent, or hold on too long after the Plateau. The secret isn't in perfect timing – it's in deep understanding.

True wealth is built not by predicting each twist, but by recognising where you are on the climb and believing in the journey.

In Terminal Value Investing, greatness isn't measured by reaching the peak, but by what comes after. The second S-curve is where legends rise again.

CHAPTER 26

Right Place, Right Time: The Luck Layer

"Ninety percent of success is just showing up."
— ***Woody Allen***

In the game of investing, skill gets you to the table. Luck keeps you there long enough to win.

While this book is grounded in frameworks, discipline, and insight, we must admit the quiet truth: luck matters. Not all luck is random — some of it is earned through awareness, preparation, and persistence. But timing, geography, and chance encounters play a larger role than we often credit.

SOMETIMES THE BIGGEST EDGE IS SIMPLY STAYING IN THE GAME.

Think of the investors who had front-row seats to inflections in liberalising India in the early '90s. Or those who clicked 'buy' on Amazon in 1997 because they were just curious. Or the early hires at Infosys, Wipro, and Zoho who received ESOPs before those acronyms meant anything.

Luck often disguises itself as timing. Being born in an economy poised for exponential growth. Working in the right city. Meeting the right mentor. Or simply surviving long enough in the market to recognise a trend.

But there's a paradox: the more prepared you are, the more often you're in the path of luck.

Investor Takeaways - Stay in the Game

Recognise the role of randomness. Respect it. Don't overattribute success to brilliance. And stay humble because in Terminal Value Investing, staying in the game often matters more than winning every hand.

CHAPTER

27

The Everest of Investing: Your Personal Summit

Epilogue

"In the short run, the market is a voting machine.
In the long run, it is a weighing machine."
— ***Benjamin Graham***

There *c*omes a point in every journey when you stop looking outward and start reflecting inward. After hundreds of pages, dozens of case studies, and countless stories of investors who held on or let go, we arrive not at someone else's summit, but at yours.

Everest isn't climbed in a quarter – it's conquered over decades.

It's the realisation that real wealth isn't made by predicting next quarter's earnings or rotating between hot sectors. It's made by backing businesses that compound over decades and holding on when everything in the market tempts you to let go.

The Terminal Value Mindset: Revisited

By now, you know the four pillars by heart:

1. Total Addressable Market: Without altitude, there is no ascent.
2. Moats: Without protection, there is no endurance.
3. Reinvestment: Without discipline, there is no flywheel.
4. Patience: Without time, there is no magic.

These aren't just tools to analyse businesses, they're lenses to see the world. Once internalised, they help you separate noise from signal, hype from durability, and price from value.

Your Personal Investing Philosophy

You've met the greats: Fisher, Munger, Buffett, Ruane, Alberg, Jhunjhunwala, and studied their philosophies. But in the end, your Everest doesn't need to be anyone else's.

- You don't need to find 50 stocks. You need one or two great ones.
- There's no need to monitor your portfolio daily.
- You don't need a CFA. You need a journal, a thesis, and patience.

True wealth is built not in bull runs, but in what you do after them. It is built by understanding business models deeply, allocating capital thoughtfully, and sitting still when others panic.

The Journey Is the Destination

- In 2002, Titan was a watchmaker ignored by institutions.
- In 1998, Infosys was dismissed as back-office labour arbitrage.
- In 1997, Amazon was an unprofitable bookstore.
- In 2007, Netflix mailed DVDs.
- In 2015, Nvidia made gaming chips, not the backbone of AI.
- In 2001, Apple was a struggling hardware company on the brink, and then came the iPod.
- In 2004, Tesla was a moon-shot EV start-up mocked by Detroit.

All these companies shared one thing: they started small, misunderstood, and underestimated. What they needed was time. And what their investors needed was clarity and conviction to hold on.

You are going to meet businesses like these again. They may look boring. Or expensive. Or out of favour. But if you can see the TAM, the Moat, the Reinvestment strategy, and the patience gap, you just might be standing at Base Camp again.

Building Your Everest Portfolio

Ask yourself:

- Do I understand this business better than most?
- Is the market underestimating its future cash flows?
- Can it reinvest at high returns for a decade or more?
- Will I be able to hold it through drawdowns, dilution and doubt?

If the answer is yes, don't just buy the stock. Buy the story. Buy the timeline. Buy the possibility that you may be early enough to capture the ascent.

Your Personal Summit

This book began with a dinner conversation in 2002. Rakesh Jhunjhunwala didn't give me a stock tip; he gave me a framework. A way to see the world not for what it is, but for what it could become. That night, Titan wasn't a jewellery retailer. It was a vehicle for compounding, trust, and patience.

That's your Everest.
That's your summit.
That's your edge.

And now, it's your turn.

Climb wisely. Climb patiently. Climb high.
The Everest of Investing awaits.

Disclaimer

This book is intended solely for educational and informational purposes. It does not constitute financial, investment, tax, legal, accounting or other professional advice. Readers should not interpret the discussions, case studies or examples herein as recommendations to buy or sell any securities or to pursue any particular investment strategy. Nothing in this book constitutes a solicitation or recommendation under any jurisdiction's securities laws.

Every effort has been made to ensure the accuracy of data, historical details and market information. However, errors or omissions may remain. Data, prices and opinions are drawn from sources believed to be reliable as of their stated dates but may change without notice. Many data points and examples are presented solely to illustrate broader concepts rather than to provide exhaustive or definitive factual records.

Any forward-looking statements or scenarios discussed are illustrative in nature, inherently uncertain, and subject to risks; actual outcomes may differ materially. Past performance of companies, markets, or investors discussed does not guarantee future results. Investing involves risk, including the possible loss of principal.

This book is an independent work and is not affiliated with, endorsed by, or sponsored by any company, organisation, or individual mentioned. All trademarks, logos, and company names remain the property of their respective owners.

The author, publisher, and associated parties disclaim any liability for losses, damages, or consequences arising from the use of this material. Investment decisions are solely the responsibility of the reader, and professional advice from a qualified financial adviser is strongly recommended.

Your Ascent Continues at EverestofInvesting.com

Every great climb has a Base Camp, a place to rest, reflect, and prepare for the next ascent.

This book is your beginning. The real climb starts when you apply its principles to your own investments.

At **EverestofInvesting.com**, you can continue your journey beyond these pages:

1. **Use the Terminal Value Software – Free**
   Build your own valuation models, estimate intrinsic value, and see how compounding unfolds through time.
2. **Explore with *Everest AI***
   Chat with an AI built on this book's full knowledge - Market Size, Moats, Reinvestment Power, Patience, and more. Learn Terminal Value Investing (TVI) with live examples. Analyse companies instantly, run long-duration DCF models, and unlock fast, TVI-driven insights that deepen your mastery.

Access through the link or QR code below.

Scan the QR or visit **EverestofInvesting.com**
to unlock **Everest AI** and the **Terminal Value Toolkit**, and start your ascent toward clarity, conviction, and compounding growth

Endnotes and References

Note on References

Each reference is cited only at its first occurrence in the book. To avoid repetition, the same source has not been listed again in subsequent chapters, even if it would otherwise be required to be referred.

Chapter 1: My Dinner with Rakesh Jhunjhunwala and the Birth of a Lifelong Idea

Titan

- Gohel, A. (2024, August 14). *The Big Bull's golden touch for Titan. LiveMint.* Retrieved August 9, 2025.
- Parikh, P. (2025, July 26). *How Rakesh Jhunjhunwala turned ₹5,000 into billions without playing it safe. The Indian Express.*

Chapter 2: Pillar 1: Market Size: The Altitude That Defines the Ascent

Microsoft

- IDC. (1986). Packaged software market size estimates [Market data table]. As cited in *In the Company of Owners: The story of the High Tech 100* (Appendix A). Rutgers University.
- International Data Corporation (IDC). (1986). Packaged software market size estimates.
- Grand View Research. (2024, March). *Cloud Computing Market Size, Share & Trends Analysis Report, 2024–2030.*
- Grand View Research. (2024). *Software Market Size, Share & Trends Industry Report, 2030.*
- Microsoft Corporation. (1986–2024). *Annual Reports (Forms 10-K).* U.S. Securities and Exchange Commission.

Titan

- World Gold Council. (2002). *Gold Demand Trends: India 2001* [PDF]. Goldhub.
- IMARC Group. (2025). *India jewellery market valuation to reach USD 150.10 billion* [Press release].
- Titan Company Limited. (2001–2025). *Annual Reports*. Titan Company.

Amazon

- U.S. Census Bureau. (2021, December 7). *Do not turn the page on bookstores*. U.S. Department of Commerce.
- Goldman Sachs. (2024). *Cloud & AI Outlook: Estimating the $2 Trillion Opportunity*.
- IMARC Group. (2024). *B2C E-Commerce Market Report (B2C Retail Classifieds)*.
- Amazon.com, Inc. (1997–2024). *Annual Reports (Forms 10-K)*. U.S. Securities and Exchange Commission.

HDFC Bank

- Reserve Bank of India. (1999). *Report on Trend and Progress of Banking in India 1998–99*.
- India Brand Equity Foundation. (2024). *Indian banking industry report*.
- HDFC Bank Limited. (1998–2025). *Annual / Integrated Annual Reports*.

Apple

- Wikipedia contributors. (n.d.). *Personal computer*. In *Wikipedia*.
- IDC. (2001). *Global PC market revenue data*.
- Goldman Sachs. (2024). *Cloud & AI Outlook and Platform Ecosystems*.
- IDC. (2024). *Global Digital Lifestyle Ecosystem Market Forecast: 2024 Edition*.
- Apple Inc. (2001–2024). *Annual Reports (Forms 10-K)*. U.S. Securities and Exchange Commission.

Kweichow Moutai

- U.S. Department of Agriculture, Foreign Agricultural Service. (2007, July 18). *China spirits market*. GAIN Report.
- Daxue Consulting. (2022, November 1). *China's spirits market: Strong demand for imported spirits*.
- CompaniesMarketCap. (2024). *Kweichow Moutai revenue*.

Infosys

- Mahnke, V., Overby, M. L., & Vang, J. (2003). *Strategic IT outsourcing: What do we know and need to know?* (Working Paper No. 2003 5). Copenhagen Business School.
- IMARC Group. (2024). *IT outsourcing market size, share, trends and forecast 2025–2033.*
- Gartner, Inc. (1999). *Forecast: Global IT Services, 1998–2003.*
- Infosys Limited. (1993–2025). *Annual Reports.*

ASML

- Chip History. (n.d.). *Building Market Share: ASML's Journey in the 1990s.*
- Global Market Insights Inc. (2024). *Lithography equipment market report, 2024–2034.*
- ASML Holding N.V. (1995–2024). *Annual Reports.*

Nvidia

- Jon Peddie Research. (2012, May 3). *PC gaming hardware market to hit $23.6 billion in 2012.*
- Jon Peddie Research. (2013, July 16). *The CG market will exceed $142 billion by 2016.*
- Huang, J. (2024, April 17). *Nvidia CEO says company has $1 trillion market opportunity.* Barron's.
- NVIDIA Corporation. (2014–2025). *Annual Reports (Forms 10-K).*

AutoZone

- The Auto Channel. (n.d.). *Automotive Aftermarket Industry Week coverage.*
- Automotive Parts Industry Association. (2011). *U.S. automotive aftermarket size 2005.* Yale EliScholar.
- Grand View Research. (2025, February). *Automotive Aftermarket Industry to Reach $489B.*
- AutoZone, Inc. (1995–2025). *Annual Reports (Forms 10-K).*

Netflix

- TVTechnology. (2004, January 12). *Consumer DVD spending increased in 2003.*

- IMARC Group. (2024). *Streaming Revolution: Top 10 Trends Shaping the OTT Market in 2025.*
- Netflix, Inc. (2002–2024). *Annual Reports (Forms 10-K).*

Monster

- Reference for Business. (n.d.). *Red Bull GmbH company profile: 2002 revenue.*
- Grand View Research. (2024, July). *Energy Drinks Market Report.*
- Monster Beverage Corporation. (2002–2025). *Annual Reports (Forms 10-K).*

Home Depot

- Butterfield, L. H. (1986, August 17). *A hardware success story: Home Depot builds on aggressive style.* Los Angeles Times.
- Home Pros Verified. (2024). *30 home improvement industry statistics & trends 2025.*
- U.S. Department of Commerce. (1982). *Current Business Reports: 1981 retail trade.*
- Home Improvement Research Institute. (2025, June 4). *HIRI U.S. Size of the Home Improvement Products Market.*
- The Home Depot, Inc. (1985–2024). *Annual Reports (Forms 10-K).*
- Research and Markets. (2024). *U.S. Home Improvement Retail Market Report 2024–2028.*

Walmart

- U.S. Census Bureau. (1976). *Statistical Abstract of the United States: 1976.*
- Walmart Inc. (1972–2024). *Annual Reports (Forms 10-K).*
- National Retail Federation. (2025, January 12). *Core retail sales grew 4% in 2024.*
- Statistics Canada. (2025, February 21). *Retail trade, December 2024.*
- Bain & Company. (2025). *How India Shops Online 2025.*

Ansys

- MSC.Software Corporation. (2001). *Registration statement on Form S-3.*
- IMARC Group. (2024). *Simulation Software Market: 2024–2032.*
- Ansys, Inc. (2000–2024). *Annual Reports (Forms 10-K).*

FICO

- U.S. Census Bureau. (2005). *Establishment and firm size: 2002.*
- The Business Research Company. (2025). *Credit bureaus global market report 2025.*
- Fair Isaac Corporation. (2002–2024). *Annual Reports (Forms 10-K).*

Eicher Motors

- Society of Indian Automobile Manufacturers (SIAM). (2007–08). *Industry Performance Report: Two-Wheelers FY 2007–08.*
- SIAM. (2024–25). *Industry Performance Report: Two-Wheelers FY 2024–25.*
- Eicher Motors Ltd. (2008–2025). *Annual / Integrated Annual Reports.*

Booking Holdings

- World Trade Organization. (n.d.). *Services sectoral classification list.*
- IMARC Group. (2025). *Online travel market: 2025–2033.*
- Booking Holdings Inc. (2000–2024). *Annual Reports (Forms 10-K).*

Bajaj Finance

- CRISIL. (2011, March). *Retail NBFC sector performance: AUM growth 2007–2010.*
- Reserve Bank of India. (2024). *Report on trend and progress of banking in India 2023–24.*
- Bajaj Finance Ltd. (2010–2025). *Annual Reports.*

Chapter 5: Pillar 3: Reinvestment Power: Multiplying Growth, Not Preserving It

Microsoft

- IDC. (1986). *Packaged software market size estimates* [Market data table]. As cited in *In the Company of Owners: The Story of the High Tech 100* (Appendix A). Rutgers University.
- International Data Corporation (IDC). (1986). *Packaged software market size estimates.*
- Grand View Research. (2024, March). *Cloud Computing Market Size, Share & Trends Analysis Report, 2024–2030.*

- Grand View Research. (2024). *Software Market Size, Share & Trends Industry Report, 2030* (global software market USD 730.70 bn in 2024; projected USD 1,397.31 bn by 2030).

Titan

- World Gold Council. (2002). *Gold Demand Trends: India 2001* [PDF]. Goldhub.
- IMARC Group. (2025). *India jewellery market valuation to reach USD 150.10 billion* [Press release].

Amazon

- U.S. Census Bureau. (2021, December 7). *Do not turn the page on bookstores*. U.S. Department of Commerce.
- Goldman Sachs. (2024). *Cloud & AI Outlook: Estimating the $2 Trillion Opportunity.*
- Wikipedia contributors. (n.d.). *Amazon Web Services*. In *Wikipedia.*
- IMARC Group. (2024). *B2C E-Commerce Market Report (B2C Retail Classifieds)*.

HDFC Bank

- Reserve Bank of India. (1999). *Financial performance of scheduled commercial banks: 1997–1999 and 1998–99 (Chapter 3)*. In *Report on Trend and Progress of Banking in India 1998–99*. Mumbai: RBI.
- India Brand Equity Foundation. (2024). *Indian banking industry report*.

Apple

- Wikipedia contributors. (n.d.). *Personal computer*. In *Wikipedia.*
- IDC. (2001). IDC reported global PC market revenue fell 13.9% in 2001 to USD 183 bn (from ~USD 213 bn in 2000).
- Goldman Sachs. (2024). *Cloud & AI Outlook and Platform Ecosystems: Market Sizing and Disruption Trends.*
- IDC. (2024). *Global Digital Lifestyle Ecosystem Market Forecast: 2024 Edition.*

Kweichow Moutai

- U.S. Department of Agriculture, Foreign Agricultural Service. (2007, July 18). *China spirits market* (GAIN Report).

- Daxue Consulting. (2022, November 1). *China's spirits market: Strong demand for imported spirits.*
- CompaniesMarketCap. (2024). *Kweichow Moutai revenue.*

Infosys

- Mahnke, V., Overby, M. L., & Vang, J. (2003). *Strategic IT outsourcing: What do we know and need to know?* (Working Paper No. 2003-5). Copenhagen Business School, Dept. of Informatics.
- IMARC Group. (2024). *IT outsourcing market size, share, trends and forecast by service model, organization size, end user, and region, 2025–2033.*
- Gartner, Inc. (1999). *Forecast: Global IT Services, 1998–2003* [Research report].

ASML

- Chip History. (n.d.). *Chapter 4: Building Market Share: ASML's Journey in the 1990s*. (Retrieved July 20, 2025).
- Global Market Insights Inc. (2024). *Lithography equipment market size, share & trend analysis report, 2024–2034*. Middleton, DE.

Nvidia

- Jon Peddie Research. (2013, July 16). *The CG market will exceed $142 billion by 2016* [Press release].
- Jon Peddie Research. (2012, May 3). *PC gaming hardware market to hit $23.6 billion in 2012* [Press release].
- Huang, J. (2024, April 17). Nvidia CEO says company has $1 trillion market opportunity. *Barron's*.
- NVIDIA Corporation. (2022). *Investor Day Presentation.*

AutoZone

- The Auto Channel. (n.d.). *Automotive Aftermarket Industry Week (AAIW) feature coverage.*
- Automotive Parts Industry Association. (2011). *U.S. automotive aftermarket reaches USD 267.6 billion in 2005*. Yale EliScholar.
- Grand View Research. (2025, February). *Automotive Aftermarket Industry to Reach $489 billion.*

Netflix

- TVTechnology. (2004, January 12). *Consumer DVD spending increased in 2003.*
- Netflix, Inc. (2003). *Form 10-K for the fiscal year ended December 31, 2002.* U.S. SEC.
- IMARC Group. (2024). *Streaming Revolution: Top 10 Trends Shaping the OTT Market in 2025.*

Monster

- Reference for Business. (n.d.). *Red Bull GmbH company profile: 2002 revenue* [Company profile].
- Grand View Research. (2024, July). *Energy Drinks Market Size, Shares, Trend Analysis Report.*

Home Depot

- Butterfield, L. H. (1986, August 17). A hardware success story: Home Depot builds on aggressive style. *Los Angeles Times.*
- Home Pros Verified. (2024). *30 home improvement industry statistics & trends in 2025* [Industry report].
- U.S. Department of Commerce, Bureau of the Census. (1982). *Current Business Reports: 1981 retail trade—Annual sales, year-end inventories, and accounts receivable, by kind of retail store (BR 81-13)* (Tables 1 & 3 for SIC 52).
- Home Improvement Research Institute. (2025, June 4). *HIRI U.S. Size of the Home Improvement Products Market.*
- Research and Markets. (2024). *U.S. Home Improvement Retail Market Report 2024–2028.*

Walmart

- U.S. Census Bureau. (1976). *Statistical Abstract of the United States: 1976* (97th ed.), Table 126 "Retail Sales by Kind of Business: 1975." Washington, DC: U.S. Dept. of Commerce.
- National Retail Federation. (2025, January 12). *Core retail sales grew 4% to a record $5.28 trillion in 2024* [Press release].
- Statistics Canada. (2025, February 21). *Retail trade, December 2024 (The Daily).*

- Bain & Company. (2025). *How India Shops Online 2025* (India e-retail ~US$60 bn in 2024, physical goods).

Ansys

- MSC.Software Corporation. (2001). *Registration statement on Form S-3*. U.S. SEC.
- IMARC Group. (2024). *Simulation Software Market: Global Industry Trends, Share, Size, Growth, Opportunity and Forecast 2024–2032*.

FICO

- U.S. Census Bureau. (2005). *Establishment and firm size: 2002* (2002 Economic Census, Subject Series; EC02-56SS-SZ) (Table 1, p. 17 shows receipts of $4,590,612,000 for credit bureaus).
- The Business Research Company. (2025). *Credit Bureaus Global Market Report 2025*.
- Fair Isaac Corporation (FICO). (2006). *Investor Day Presentation: Fiscal Year 2005*.

Eicher Motors

- SIAM. (2007–08). *Industry Performance Report: Two-Wheelers FY 2007–08*.
- SIAM. (2024–25). *Industry Performance Report: Two-Wheelers FY 2024–25*.

Booking Holdings

- World Trade Organization. (n.d.). *Results of the Uruguay Round of multilateral trade negotiations: Services sectoral classification list*.
- IMARC Group. (2025). *Online travel market: Size, share, trends and forecast 2025–2033*.

Bajaj Finance

- CRISIL. (2011, March). *Retail NBFC sector performance: AUM growth 2007–2010 (Compendium)*.
- Reserve Bank of India. (2024). *Report on Trend and Progress of Banking in India 2023–24*.

Chapter 5: Pillar 3: Reinvestment Power: Multiplying Growth, Not Preserving It

Microsoft

- Microsoft Corporation. (2016, Feb 24). *Microsoft acquires Xamarin...* [Press release].
- Greene, J. (2016, Feb 24). Microsoft agrees to acquire Xamarin (est. $400–$500 m). *The Wall Street Journal.*
- Microsoft Corporation. (2016, Jun 13). *Microsoft to acquire LinkedIn for $26.2 bn* [Press release].
- Microsoft Corporation. (2018, Jun 4). *Microsoft to acquire GitHub for $7.5 bn* [Press release].
- Microsoft Corporation. (2021, Apr 12). *Microsoft... acquisition of Nuance* [Press release].
- Associated Press. (2023, October 13). Microsoft closes deal to buy Call of Duty maker Activision Blizzard after antitrust fights. *AP News.*
- Microsoft Corporation. (2024, Jul 30). *Azure revenue tops $75 bn, FY24* [Earnings release].
- Macrotrends LLC. (2025). *Microsoft operating margin 2010–2025.*
- Foley, M. J. (2008, Oct 27). Microsoft's cloud OS is Windows Azure. *ZDNet.*
- Microsoft Corporation. (2008, Oct 27). *Microsoft unveils Windows Azure* [Press release].
- Foley, M. J. (2010, Jan 4). Microsoft to launch Azure on Feb 1, 2010. *ZDNet.*
- Microsoft Corporation. (2010, Feb 1). *Windows Azure platform now commercially available* [Press release].
- Foley, M. J. (2014, Mar 25). Microsoft renames Windows Azure to Microsoft Azure. *ZDNet.*

Titan (Reinvestment in jewellery retail)

- Titan Company Limited. (2025, May). *Q4 FY25 earnings presentation.1.*
- Mukund, A. (2001). *Tanishq: The turnaround story* [Case study]. ICMR India.

Amazon (Relentless reinvestment)

- Amazon Web Services. (2006, Mar 14). *AWS launches Amazon S3* [Press release].
- Amazon.com, Inc. (2025, Feb 6). *Amazon.com announces fourth quarter results* [Press release].
- Fifth Person. (2025, Mar 13). *Amazon Q4 2024 earnings call: AWS margin drivers.*

- *Financial Times*. (2024). *Amazon cloud sales growth accelerates...*
- Whitten, S. (2017, Jun 16). Amazon buying Whole Foods for $13.7 bn. *CNBC*.

HDFC Bank (technology & branch digitization/mergers)

- HDFC Bank Ltd. (2000, Feb 26). *Merger with Times Bank—stock-for-stock* [Annual report note].
- HDFC Bank Ltd. (2008, Feb 25). *Merger with Centurion Bank of Punjab* [Press release].

Kweichow Moutai (capacity & brand heritage)

- Bocconi Chinese Student Association. (2025, June 19). *Kweichow Moutai: The spirit that leads the market.*

ASML (R&D intensity, M&A)

- ASML. (n.d.). *Annual reports and financial statements (1996–2024).*
- ASML Holding N.V. (2000, Oct 2). *To acquire Silicon Valley Group Inc.* [Press release].

AutoZone (logistics, DIFM, acquisitions)

- AutoZone, Inc. (1996, Feb 27). *Acquires ALLDATA Corporation.*
- AutoZone, Inc. (1998, Jun 8). *To acquire Chief Auto Parts for $280 m* [Press release].
- AutoZone, Inc. (1998, Aug 24). *Completes acquisition of TruckPro L.P.*
- AutoZone, Inc. (1998, Sep 15). *Completes acquisition of Auto Palace* [PR Newswire].
- AutoZone, Inc. (2012, Dec 27). *Acquires AutoAnything.com* [PR Newswire].

Home Depot (stores, supply chain, Pro)

- Wikipedia contributors. (n.d.). *Home Depot*. (Retrieved Aug 2025).
- *The New Yorker*. (2012, Apr 30). *Building Business*.

Walmart (tech, supply chain, omni, global)

- Wikipedia contributors. (2025, Aug 13). *Walmart.*
- *LiveMint*. (2018, May 9). *Walmart buys Flipkart for $16 bn.*

Ansys (workflow integration & M&A)

- Ansys Inc. (2001). *Acquires ICEM CFD.*
- Ansys Inc. (2003). *Announces acquisition of CFX.*
- Ansys Inc. (2006, Feb 28). *To acquire Fluent Incorporated for $565 m.*

FICO (data & analytics platform, M&A)

- Fair Isaac Corporation. (2002, Apr 29). *To merge with HNC Software* [Press release].
- Fair Isaac Corporation. (2004, Sep 21). *Fair Isaac and Braun Consulting acquisition* [Press release].
- Fair Isaac Corporation. (2012, Nov 26). *FICO acquires CR Software.*
- Fair Isaac Corporation. (2013, Apr 1). *FICO acquires Infoglide Software.*
- Fair Isaac Corporation. (2018, Dec 12). *FICO acquires GoOn* (Brazil).

Royal Enfield / Eicher (culture, capacity, global)

- Eicher Motors Limited. (2019). *Annual Report 2019* (One Ride event; Oragadam & Vallam Vadagal plants).
- Wikipedia contributors. (2025, Aug). *Royal Enfield.*

Additional datapoints used in this chapter

- Trefis. (2025). *Breaking Down Apple's Services Revenue.*
- AlphaQuery. (n.d.). *NVIDIA Corp (NVDA) operating profit margin (annual).*
- Hansen Natural (2003) Form 10-K FY2002;
- Monster–Coca-Cola partnership (2014, Aug 14) [Press release].
- Microsoft Corporation. (2024, Jul 30). *Intelligent Cloud performance: FY24 Q4 earnings.*
- Tom's Hardware. (2025, Jul 20). *Microsoft surpasses $4 trn market cap on AI demand.*
- GuruFocus. (2025, Apr 29). *Booking Holdings facilitates $1.8 bn stock buyback.*
- Bajaj Finance Limited. (2025, Jul 17). *Q1 FY26 international investor presentation.*

Booking Holdings (precision reinvestment)

- PhocusWire. (2018, Apr 19). *Booking Holdings buys FareHarbor.*
- PhocusWire. (2013, May 21). *Priceline acquires KAYAK for $1.8 bn.*

- Skift. (2005, Jul 1). *Priceline.com acquires Booking.com.*
- GuruFocus. (2025). *BKNG Q4 2024 holdings and buybacks.*

Bajaj Finance (growing faster)

- Bajaj Finance Limited. (2011). *Investor Presentation FY11* (AUM: ₹ 24.78 bn FY08; ₹ 40.32 bn FY10).

Chapter 9: Base Camp

Microsoft (2008-2016): From desktop to cloud

- Wikipedia contributors. (2025). *Microsoft Azure.*
- Goldman Sachs. (2024, Sep 11). *Cloud computing to hit $2 trn by 2030; gen-AI to drive growth. The AI Insider.*
- Microsoft Corporation. (2024, Mar 14). *Microsoft and Oracle expand partnership for Oracle Database@Azure.*
- *TIME.* (2015, Apr 16). *Satya Nadella joins TIME 100.*
- Microsoft. (2016, Feb 24). *Acquires Xamarin.*
- Microsoft. (2016, Jun 13). *To acquire LinkedIn.*

Titan (2001-2008): Building the gold standard

- Wikipedia contributors. (2025). *Tanishq.*
- Dogra, K. (2020). *A case study on Tanishq.*
- Wikipedia contributors. (2025). *Tanishq.*

Amazon (2001-2009): Building the flywheel

- Wikipedia contributors. (2025). *History of Amazon.*

HDFC Bank (2000-2008): Retail backbone

- HDFC Bank. (n.d.). *Who we are: Mergers & Distribution network.*
- HDFC (Housing Development Finance Corporation). (n.d.). *CBoP & Times Bank amalgamation.*
- Wikipedia contributors. (2025, Jul). *HDFC Bank.*

Apple

- Artnet News. (2022, May 17). *What the end of the iPod reveals…*

- Apple. (2005, Jun 6). *Apple to use Intel microprocessors beginning in 2006* [Press release].

Kweichow Moutai (2003–2010)

- CompaniesMarketCap. (2024). *Kweichow Moutai revenue.*
- USDA FAS. (2007, Jul 18). *China spirits market* (GAIN).

Infosys

- Infosys Technologies Limited. (1999, Dec 2). *Infosys announces SEI CMM Level 5...* [Press release].

ASML (1996–2003)

- ASML. (n.d.). *History.*
- Wikipedia contributors. (2025, Jan 8). *ASML Holding.*
- Intel Corporation. (2009, Mar 2). *Intel Capital & VCs invest in ASML for EUV.*
- ASML Holding N.V. (2003, Dec 18). *ASML and Samsung sign global IP licensing agreement.*

NVIDIA (2010–2016)

- NVIDIA. (2010, Sep 22). *Expands CUDA developer ecosystem.* NVIDIA Newsroom.

AutoZone (1995–2001)

- AutoZone, Inc. (n.d.). *Our history & timeline.*
- *Restructuring Newsletter.* (2024, Aug 2). *AutoZone deep dive.*

Netflix (2002–2010)

- MIDiA Research. (2017, Jan 16). *Netflix and the tenth anniversary of video streaming.*

Monster (1998–2008)

- *Business Outreach India.* (2025, Feb 11). *How Monster Beverage became a market leader.*

- In Practise. (2022, Feb 7). *Monster, Fever-Tree and non-alcoholic beverage distribution.*

Home Depot (1985–1990)

- Home Depot. (1986). *Annual Report 1985 (p. XX).*
- University of Alabama, Birmingham. (1990). *Home Depot corporate history overview.*

Walmart (1975–1985)

- Wikipedia contributors. (2025). *History of Walmart.*

Ansys (2000–2007)

- ANSYS, Inc. (2003, Feb 4). *ANSYS to acquire CFX...* SEC archive.
- Wikipedia contributors. (2025). *ANSYS.*

FICO (2000–2007)

- *Fintech Takes.* (2024, Jan 12). *The (Unlikely) End of the FICO Score.*

Eicher Motors: Royal Enfield (2005–2010)

- *Economic Times.* (2015, Mar 5). *Meet Siddhartha Lal... turned around Royal Enfield.*

Booking Holdings (2000–2007)

- Priceline.com. (2004, Sep 21). *Acquires Active Hotels.*
- Priceline.com. (2005, Jul 14). *Acquires Bookings B.V.*
- Wikipedia contributors. (2025, Aug). *Booking.com.*

Bajaj Finance (2008–2013)

- CapitalMarket.com. (n.d.). *Bajaj Auto Finance's transition into diversified lending.*
- Wikipedia contributors. (2025). *Sanjiv Bajaj.*

Chapter 11: Optionality and Second Base Camp

Apple

- Apple Inc. (2025, Jun 5). *Global App Store helps developers reach new heights... $1.3 trn in 2024* [Press release].
- *FinTech Magazine*. (2023, Jul 10). *The App Store turns 15: Apple's digital revolution.*
- Apple Inc. (2023, May 31). *Developers generated $1.1 trn in the App Store ecosystem in 2022.*
- *Wired*. (2024, Apr 24). *The Apple Watch turns 10—and it's more important than ever.*
- *Forbes*. (2025, Apr 10). *The growing value of wearables.*

Microsoft

- Microsoft. (2025, Jul 24). *Microsoft Cloud strength drives fourth quarter results.*
- Microsoft. (2016, Jun 13). *To acquire LinkedIn for $26.2 bn.*
- Microsoft. (2018, Jun 4). *To acquire GitHub for $7.5 bn.*
- Microsoft. (2017, Mar 14). *Teams now generally available in Office 365.*
- Microsoft. (2023, Jan 23). *Microsoft and OpenAI extend partnership.*

Netflix

- Netflix, Inc. (2011). *Form 10-K for year ended December 31, 2010.* U.S. SEC.
- Wikipedia contributors. (2025). *Netflix — Historical financials and membership growth.*

Coca-Cola

- Wikipedia contributors. (2025). *The Coca-Cola Company.*
- Business Wire. (2018, Aug 14). *The Coca-Cola Company and BODYARMOR announce new strategic relationship.*
- Onwish.ai. (2023). *Coca-Cola's growth strategy: Innovations and market expansion.*

Amazon

- HighRadius. (2025). *Amazon's financial growth: Assets, liabilities & AWS profits.*
- Investopedia. (2025). *How Amazon makes money.*

- *TIME*. (2025). *Why AWS CEO Matt Garman is playing the long game on AI.*
- TechRadar Pro. (2025). *Amazon's data center spend tops $100 bn.*
- FourWeekMBA. (2024, Feb 22). *AWS revenues 2013–2023.*

Nvidia

- *Business Insider*. (2025, Jun 13). *Ian Buck built Nvidia's secret weapon...*
- AInvest. (2025, Jul 17). *Nvidia's ecosystem dominance and AI market consolidation.*
- Wikipedia contributors. (2025). *Nvidia.*

Titan

- ScrapeHero. (2025, Apr 4). *Number of Tanishq locations in India.*
- StockGro. (2025, Apr 8). *Kalyan Jewellers vs Tanishq: Which is better?*

Chapter 12: Changing Customer Behaviour: The Hidden Engine of TAM Expansion

Infosys

- *Wired*. (2003, July 1). *The Wired 40: Infosys: Coders without borders.*

Apple

- Apple. (2007, Jan 9). *Apple reinvents the phone with iPhone* [Press release].

Amazon: Retail norms

- Wikipedia contributors. (n.d.). *Amazon (company).*

Netflix

- Wikipedia contributors. (2025, Aug 25). *Netflix.*

Titan (Tanishq): Professionalizing jewellery

- Wikipedia contributors. (2025). *Tanishq* (first organized chain; transparency/ purity testing).

Walmart: Democratizing affordability

- Britannica. (n.d.). *Walmart | History & facts* (Britannica Money).
- *YourStory*. (2024, Dec). *The Walmart Way: Dream Big, Discount Bigger.*

Home Depot: DIY culture

- Encyclopedia.com. (2025). *Do-it-yourself philosophy of The Home Depot.*
- Britannica. (n.d.). *The Home Depot | History, growth, & the DIY revolution.*

Booking Holdings: DIY travel as default

- World Trade Organization. (n.d.). *Services sectoral classification list.*
- IMARC Group. (2025). *Online travel market: 2025–2033.*

Bajaj Finance: Credit becomes aspirational

- CRISIL. (2011, Mar). *Retail NBFC sector performance: AUM growth 2007–2010.*
- RBI. (2024). *Report on Trend and Progress of Banking in India 2023–24.*

Chapter 14: From Unit Economics to Terminal Value

Amazon

- Amazon.com, Inc. (2025, Feb 6). *Amazon.com announces fourth quarter results* [Press release].
- Petrov, D. (2024, Oct 4). *Apple earns 60% gross margin on the iPhone 16 Pro Max... PhoneArena.*

Chapter 15: The Blind Spot: Why Most Models Never Catch the 100x Climb

- S-Curve Verschuur, M. (2011). The S-curve: An analysis of the impact of technological progress on organizational performance. Tilburg University.

Chapter 16: The Costliest Exit — Why Most Investors Sell Too Soon

Carl Icahn & Netflix

- U.S. SEC. (2012). *Icahn Capital L.P. Schedule 13D for Netflix, Inc.*
- CNBC. (2013, Oct 1). Icahn sells half of Netflix stake—"fully valued."

Howard Marks & Apple

- Marks, H. (2023). *Fewer Losers, or More Winners?* Oaktree Capital Management.

Peter Lynch & Taco Bell

- Lynch, P. (1994). Interview with Karmin. MOI Global.

Suze Orman & Amazon

- Orman, S. (2018, Oct 10). Selling Amazon stock is my No. 1 money regret. *Yahoo Finance.*
- Moneywise. (n.d.). Famous investors share their biggest investing regrets.

Warren Buffett & Disney

- Belmonte, J. (2024, May 20). Warren Buffett's blunders: 3 investments... *Yahoo Finance.*
- Berkshire Hathaway Inc. (1995). *1995 Shareholder Letter.*
- CNBC. (2009, May 4). Warren Buffett: The $10 B Disney mistake.

Sequoia Capital & Apple

- The Hustle. (2020, November 25). *The story of Sequoia, a Silicon Valley VC legend.* The Hustle.
- Sequoia Capital. (2021, Oct). *The Sequoia Fund: Patient capital...*

Yahoo & Alibaba

- Arthur, C., & Agencies. (2012, Sep 19). Yahoo sells chunk of Alibaba stake. *The Guardian.*

- Oreskovic, A. (2018, Apr 18). Marissa Mayer blames short-sighted activist investors... *Business Insider.*

Peter Thiel & Facebook

- Garside, J. (2012, Aug 21). Peter Thiel cashes in Facebook shares. *The Guardian.*
- Mukherjee, S. (2017, Nov 22). Peter Thiel sells most of remaining Facebook stake. *Reuters.*
- Arthur, C. (2012, Aug 21). Facebook director Peter Thiel sells majority... *The Guardian.*

SoftBank & Nvidia

- Fujikawa, M. (2024, Jun 21). SoftBank chief rues selling Nvidia stake... *Financial News London.*
- Wikipedia contributors. (2025). SoftBank Vision Fund.
- Benzinga. (2024, Jun 25). The $150 bn opportunity SoftBank lost...

Chapter 17: Patience Premium: The Legendary Investors Who Let Times do Heavy Lifting.

Rakesh Jhunjhunwala

- Gohel, A. (2024, Aug 14). The Big Bull's golden touch for Titan. *LiveMint.*
- Parikh, P. (2025, Jul 26). RJ turned ₹5,000 into billions... *The Indian Express.*

Chuck Akre

- My Investing Daily. (n.d.). My evening with Chuck Akre: Part 2.
- American Tower Corporation. (2001–2024). *Annual Reports (Forms 10-K).* U.S. Securities and Exchange Commission
- GuruFocus. (2019, Jan 2). Guru Profile: Chuck Akre's path to success.

Nick Sleep

- Sleep, N., & Zakaria, Q. (2014). *Nomad Investment Partnership letters (2001–2014).* The I.G.Y. Foundation.

- Karlsson, K. (2023, Sep 28). Nomad's Costco investment. *Quartr.*
- Nour, C. (2024). Nick Sleep: The master of compounders. *Stock Unlock Newsletter.*

Philip Fisher

- Fisher, P. A. (1996). *Common Stocks and Uncommon Profits and Other Writings* (Rev. ed.). Wiley. (Original 1958)
- Train, J. (2000). *The New Money Masters.* Harper Business.
- Investopedia. (n.d.). Philip Fisher: History, market impact, FAQs.
- Motorola, Inc. (1956). *1956 Motorola annual report.* Retrieved from Motorola Solutions corporate archive
- Motorola Solutions, Inc. (2005, March 4). *Motorola Solutions annual report 2004.* Retrieved from Motorola Solutions corporate archivesWarren Buffett
- Trustnet Learn. (2025, May 2). Warren Buffett and Coca-Cola.
- Business Insider News. (2025, May). Buffett hails Tim Cook…
- Business Insider. (2025, May 5). Best and worst investments.
- Zieminski, N. (2009, Nov 3). Buying Burlington Northern. *Reuters.*
- Nasdaq. (2022, Mar 31). Buffett's 3 greatest investments.
- Reuters. (2022, Aug 30). Berkshire paid $232 m; value ~$7.5 bn.
- Buffett, W. E. (2019). *Berkshire Hathaway Letters to Shareholders (1965–2018).*
- Trustnet Ltd. (2025, May 30). Buffett and American Express.
- Moomoo Technologies. (2024, Jan 27). American Express dividend increase
- Business Insider. (2019, Jul 12). See's Candies — Buffett's favorite.
- Reuters. (2024, Jun 17). Berkshire trims BYD.
- Reuters. (2022, Aug 30). Berkshire paid $232 m; value ~$7.5 bn.
- Berkshire Hathaway. (2023). *2022 Annual Letter to Shareholders* [PDF

Peter Lynch

- Wikipedia contributors. (2025). Peter Lynch.
- Wharton Magazine. (n.d.). Stock Superstar… Peter S. Lynch.
- Lynch, P., & Rothchild, J. (1994, 2000). *Beating the Street; One Up on Wall Street.*
- Curzio Research. (2023, March 15). *Peter Lynch's greatest investment ever: A critical lesson for the bearish landscape.* Curzio Research
- YouTube. (2018, June 17). *Peter Lynch's love for volatility and the Taco Bell investment* [Video]. YouTube.
- Reuters. (2005, December 12). *Dunkin' Donuts, Baskin-Robbins sold for $2.43 billion.* Reuters.
- PBS. (1996). *Interview with Peter Lynch* [Transcript]. In *Frontline: Betting on the market.* PBS. Retrieved

Thomas Russo

- GuruFocus. (2024). Thomas Russo's top holdings and performance.
- Tom A. Russo. (2013, April 10). *Musings on "Global Value" Equity Investing* [PowerPoint slides]. Richard Ivey School of Business.

Li Lu

- Wikipedia contributors. (2025, January 22). *Himalaya Capital.* In *Wikipedia.*
- Franck, T. (2023, September 14). Charlie Munger's protégé Li Lu made him a fortune on BYD. *Business Insider.*

Ron Baron

- Reuters. (2023, Sep 13; Nov 10). Baron's SpaceX stake; SpaceX worth ~$500 bn by 2030.
- Morningstar. (2022). Baron Partners Fund (BPTRX) Performance Summary.
- Franck, T. (2025, March 11). *Ron Baron says he won't sell a single personal Tesla share despite nosedive.* CNBC.

Charlie Munger

- Ashworth, W. (2023, Nov 29). Best bet: Berkshire vs Costco? *Nasdaq.*
- Stone, D. (2025, Mar 14). Why Munger never sold Costco. *Yahoo Finance.*
- Wikipedia contributors. (2024, Jul 15). Charlie Munger.

Raamdeo Agrawal

- Alpha Ideas. (2016, Aug 9). A famous investment.

Chapter 19: The Century Club — Where Arithmetic Becomes Alchemy

- Stock price data: Yahoo Finance (retrieved 2025).

Chapter 20: The Greatest Sip of All Time — "One Share. One Century. $28 Million."

- Nasdaq. (2020, Dec 6). A $120 investment in Coca-Cola's IPO would be worth…
- GuruFocus. (2012, Mar 24). The Coca-Cola Company: 1920–1924.

- The Coca-Cola Company. (n.d.). *History: The chronicle of Coca-Cola.*
- The Coca-Cola Company. (n.d.). *Diet Coke: A global brand premiere (1982).*
- Investopedia. (2016, Jan 12). 5 companies owned by Coca-Cola.
- Wikipedia contributors. (2025). The Coca-Cola Company.
- The Coca-Cola Company. (2025, Feb 13). Q4 and full-year 2024 results.
- cInvestopedia. (2015, May 26). Why did Warren Buffett invest heavily in Coca-Cola in the late 1980s?
- The Coca-Cola Company. (n.d.). *Annual filings (Form 10-K).*

Chapter 21: Lesson from History - 1991: The Year India Unlocked Terminal Value

- Plutus IAS. (2023). Hindu rate of growth and India's economic reforms.
- Wikipedia contributors. (2025). Economic liberalisation in India.
- Economic Times. (2024, Dec 30). Manmohan Singh: One surprising phone call in 1991 that changed India's economy.

Chapter 22: Legacy Builders: Founders and Leaders Who Thought in Decades

(Wikipedia first appearances already retained in earlier chapters; here only new leaders)

- Wikipedia contributors. (2025). Warren Buffett; Jeff Bezos; Elon Musk; Bernard Arnault; N. R. Narayana Murthy; Satya Nadella; Bob Iger; Jensen Huang; Bajaj Group; Wang Chuanfu; Sam Walton; Larry Ellison; Deepak Parekh; Dhirubhai Ambani; Sunil Bharti Mittal; Ingvar Kamprad; Amancio Ortega; Bill Gates; Steve Jobs; Frederick W. Smith; John C. Bogle; Howard Schultz; Ray Kroc; Jim Sinegal; Phil Knight; Enzo Ferrari; Leonardo Del Vecchio; Hans Wilsdorf; Marc Benioff; Reed Hastings; Charles R. Schwab; Ken Langone; Jack Dorsey; Murali Divi.

Bernard Arnault: The Keeper of Timelessness

- Tungate, M. (2009). *Luxury world: The past, present and future of luxury brands*. Kogan Page.
- **Columb, F. (2023). *Bernard Arnault: The making of the world's richest*** *man*. Hodder & Stoughton

Satya Nadella: The Culture Reformer

- Nadella, S., & Shaw, G. (2017). *Hit refresh: The quest to rediscover Microsoft's soul and imagine a better future for everyone*. Harper Business.

Bob Iger: The Strategist of Storytelling

- Iger, B., & Penn, M. (2019). *The ride of a lifetime: Lessons learned from 15 years as CEO of the Walt Disney Company*. Random House

Wang Chuanfu: The Chemist Who Electrified the Future

- White, J. (2024, July 10). *How BYD overtook Tesla in China's EV market. Reuters*.
- Kamprad, I., & Bjurström, C. (2014). *Leading by design: The IKEA story*. Penguin Random House.

Amancio Ortega: Fast Fashion's Reluctant Billionain

- Lopez, J., & Ortega, A. (2015). *The Inditex way: Zara and the rise of fast fashion*. Penguin Random House.

Bill Gates: Architect of the Software Century

- Gates, B., & Myhrvold, N. (1995). *The road ahead*. Viking.

Steve Jobs: The Perfectionist Who Made Technology Beautiful

- Isaacson, W. (2011). *Steve Jobs*. Simon & Schuster

John Bogle: Democratizer of Wealth:

- Bogle, J. C. (2017). *The little book of common sense investing: The only way to guarantee your fair share of stock market returns* (10th anniversary ed.). Wiley.
- Vanguard. (2025, February 3). *Vanguard announces largest ever expense ratio reduction; savings of more than $350 million in 2025*. Valley Forge, PA
- Trangle, S. (2025, February 3). *Vanguard chops fees across 87 mutual funds, ETFs*. Investopedia.

Howard Schultz: Brewing Culture at Scale

- Schultz, H., & Yang, D. J. (2011). *Onward: How Starbucks fought for its life without losing its soul*. Rodale Books.

- Starbucks Corporation. (2023, August 1). *Q3 2023 earnings call (Corrected transcript).* FactSet CallStreet.
- GeekWire. (2024, January 31). *Starbucks mobile orders surpass 30% of total transactions at U.S. stores for the first time.*

Ray Kroc: Master of Scale and System

- Kroc, R., & Anderson, R. (1977). *Grinding it out: The making of McDonald's.* St. Martin's Press.
- McDonald's Corporation. (2025, September 9). *Purpose & Impact progress report 2024–2025* (states "serving 70 million customers" and operations in 100+ countries).

Jim Sinegal: Frugal Genius of Wholesale Trust

- Sinegal, J., & Fishman, C. (2003). *The Costco way: Lessons in value and culture.* Crown Business.
- Costco Wholesale Corporation. (2019). *Form 10-K for the fiscal year ended September 1, 2019.* U.S. Securities and Exchange Commission.
- Food Industry Association. (n.d.). *Food industry facts.*
- Costco Customer Service. (2024, September 1). *Membership fee increase.*

Phil Knight: Building Identity Through Performance

- Knight, P., & Strasser, B. (2016). *Shoe dog: A memoir by the creator of Nike.* Scribner.

Enzo Ferrari: Engineering Desire, Not Just Speed

- Ferrari, E., & Sobiella, R. (2007). *Ferrari: The legend.* Giorgio Nada Editore

Leonardo Del Vecchio: Invisible Eyewear Emperor

- Del Vecchio, L., & Capellini, P. (2018). *Luxottica: The making of a global eyewear empire.* Baldini & Castoldi.

Hans Wilsdorf: Custodian of Horological Permanence

- Wilsdorf, H., & Baillie, J. (2007). *Rolex: The story of the world's most prestigious watch.* Assouline.

Marc Benioff: Champion of Cloud and Conscience

- Benioff, M., & Adler, C. (2009). *Behind the cloud: The untold story of how Salesforce.com went from idea to billion-dollar company-and revolutionized an industry*. Jossey-Bass.

Reed Hastings: Architect of On-Demand Entertainment

- Hastings, R., & Meyer, E. (2020). *No rules rules: Netflix and the culture of reinvention*. Penguin Press.
- Netflix, Inc. (2025, January 21). *Q4 2024 shareholder letter.*

Chuck Schwab: Broker for Main Street

- V YourLastName, Y. (2025). *Post-1975 deregulation, Schwab launched a discount brokerage...* [Unpublished manuscript].
- Schwab, C., & Adams, J. (2005). *Charles Schwab: How one man revolutionized investing*. John Wiley & Sons.

Ken Langone: Merchant Who Empowered the Masses

- Langone, B., & Meehan, T. (1999). *The Home Depot story: How a small startup became a retail giant*. Crown Business.
- The Home Depot, Inc. (2025). *Form 10-K for the fiscal year ended February 2, 2025.* U.S. Securities and Exchange Commission.

Murali Divi: Silent Chemist of Global APIs

- *Laboratories specialised in complex APIs...* [Unpublished manuscript].
- Investment Company Institute. (2025, August 29). *Active and index combined long-term mutual funds and ETFs*

Chapter 23: The Summit — How to Recognize It, and What to Do

- Wikipedia contributors. (n.d.). History of IBM: Personal computer era and DOS licensing.
- The Procter & Gamble Company. (2000–2025). *Annual Reports.*
- Nestlé S.A. (2000–2025). *Annual Reports.*

Index

N

O

P